Martha D. L. Haynie

English Syntax and Analysis

Simplified

Martha D. L. Haynie

English Syntax and Analysis
Simplified

ISBN/EAN: 9783742812520

Manufactured in Europe, USA, Canada, Australia, Japa

Cover: Foto ©Andreas Hilbeck / pixelio.de

Manufactured and distributed by brebook publishing software (www.brebook.com)

Martha D. L. Haynie

English Syntax and Analysis

ENGLISH SYNTAX AND ANALYSIS

SIMPLIFIED.

DESIGNED FOR USE IN COMMON SCHOOLS, HIGH SCHOOLS, AND NORMAL SCHOOLS.

BY

MRS. M. D. L. HAYNIE,

Professor of Modern Languages, Illinois State Normal University.

CHICAGO:
GEO. SHERWOOD & CO.

Copyright, 1884,
By GEO. SHERWOOD & CO.,
CHICAGO.

To
MY PUPILS,
WHO ARE NOW IN AMERICA, EUROPE, AND THE ISLES OF THE SEA,
THIS BOOK IS DEDICATED
BY THE AUTHORESS,
AS A TOKEN OF AFFECTIONATE REMEMBRANCE, FOR THEIR UNVARYING KINDNESS, AND FULL APPRECIATION OF HER LABORS AMONG THEM.

PREFACE.

This book appears before the public, in answer to many calls.

For years my pupils, and, also, teachers whom I have never known personally, have urged me to embody my teaching in book form, so that they could put into the hands of their own pupils, a text-book, attractive, easy of comprehension, and at the same time scholarly.

Cheerfully, but not without labor, the task has been performed, and the book is now sent forth on its mission, without a misgiving of its success, wherever it may happen to find a welcome.

Syntax and Analysis are treated together, as they are so closely related, it is difficult to treat them separately.

In simplifying these difficult subjects, no element has been omitted, but into the work have entered deep thought, and the result of the careful and extended research of years.

A very long experience in teaching modern languages, has enabled me to understand the difficulties to be met with at every step, when undertaking the study of, even the mother-tongue, and from this experience has resulted the plan of this work.

Step by step the pupil is led from the simple to the abstruse.

PREFACE.

The simple sentence is treated in full; first, without any modifier, and afterwards, with the modifiers, in methodical order, before the complex sentence is introduced; and the complex sentence is exhaustively treated, before the compound sentence is introduced.

Abundant and full analyses are given as models; and no kind of sentence is omitted.

The uses of the verb *Be*, the copulative verbs, and transitive and intransitive verbs, are fully explained, but no special reference is made to auxiliary verbs, as they are fully treated of in my Etymology, soon to be published.

The book should not be put into the hands of any who have not a fair knowledge of Etymology; for, in order to construct sentences, a knowledge of words and their uses is absolutely necessary.

Thanks are due to the grammars in whose companionship I have lived from my childhood; and to the kind friends whose commendatory words have encouraged me all along the way.

MARTHA D. L. HAYNIE.

Illinois State Normal University,
  March 22, 1884.

CONTENTS.

	PAGE
SYNTAX,—DEFINITIONS AND EXPLANATIONS,	9–12
ELEMENTS OF THE SENTENCE; SENTENCES CLASSIFIED BY USE AND BY STRUCTURE,	12–18
ANALYSIS DEFINED,	19
THE SIMPLE SENTENCE IN ALL ITS FORMS, AND WITH ALL THE MODIFIERS BELONGING TO IT,	19–91
RULES OF SYNTAX,	92–94
RULES OF ANALYSIS,	94–96
THE CLAUSE ELEMENT,	97–105
COMPLEX SENTENCES,	105–202
ADJECTIVE CLAUSES,	106–126
OBJECTIVE CLAUSES,	127–135
ADVERBIAL CLAUSES,	136–202
ABRIDGED PROPOSITIONS,	203–208
COMPOUND SENTENCES,	209–243
CONDENSED OR PARTIALLY COMPOUND SENTENCES,	243–248
IDIOMATIC CONSTRUCTIONS,	149–150
MODELS FOR ANALYSIS, OUTLINE ANALYSIS, AND EXERCISE UPON EXCLAMATORY SENTENCES,	251–271

SYNTAX.

The ***division*** of ***grammar*** which treats of ***sentence-making*** is called *Syntax*.

The word ***Syntax*** is derived from two Greek words, ***syn,*** together, and ***taxis,*** arrangement.

Sentences are composed of ***words,*** therefore:

Syntax *is the correct use, and the methodical arrangement of words in the construction of sentences.*

False Syntax *is the incorrect use, or the faulty arrangement of words in the construction of a sentence.*

A ***sentence*** *is the expression of a* ***thought*** *in words.*

A ***thought*** *is a collection of ideas making complete sense in the mind, before it is expressed.*

An ***idea*** *is a* ***mental picture.***

Every ***sentence*** must contain at least one ***proposition.***

A ***proposition*** *consists of a combination of words, forming a statement.*

In a proposition, two ***terms*** are necessary:

1.—***Subject.***
2.—***Predicate.***

Therefore: *A proposition is the combination of a subject and a predicate.*

The **Subject** *of a proposition is the word, or words, used to represent that of which something is said or affirmed.*

The **Predicate** *of a proposition is the word, or words, used to represent that which is said or affirmed of the subject.*

Ex.—*Rain falls.*

In this *proposition*, the word *Rain* represents that about which *something* is *said* or *affirmed*, therefore it is the subject, or first *term* of the *proposition*.

The *subject* must be a *noun* or a *pronoun*, or something used as such.

A *symbol*, a *figure*, a *letter*, a *phrase* or a *clause*, may be used to represent *that about which something* is said, and thus become the *subject* of a proposition.

A *phrase* (as a grammatical term), consists of *a preposition and its object*, or *an infinitive*, with the sign *to*, either expressed or understood.

A *clause* is the combination of a *subject* and a *predicate* (a proposition) used as an *element* of a *sentence*.

Ex. 1.—*Mary* sings.
    2.—*He* reads.
    3.—+ is the sign of Addition.
    4.—*7* is a figure.
    5.—*H* is a letter.
    6.—*To retire from business* is his intention.
    7.—*That you are so careless* surprises me.

There are many *complete sentences* which contain neither a *noun* nor a *pronoun*.

Such *sentences* have for their *subject*, either a *phrase* or *clause*, used substantively.

Ex.—*To submit now* would be humiliating.

That to live happily is not impossible has been proved positively, and very frequently.

The **simple** or **grammatical subject** is the *word, phrase* or *clause* taken alone.

The **complex** or **logical subject** is the *word, phrase* or *clause* taken with the modifiers.

In the following sentence:

An *industrious, prudent boy* will succeed, the word *boy* is the *simple* or *grammatical* subject, and the words, *An industrious, prudent boy* is the *complex* or *logical* subject.

The *Predicate* must contain a *verb*. No other part of speech can take its place; for no other part of speech has the *power* to make an *assertion*.

It is frequently the case, however, that other words, called **attributes** of the subject, combine with the verb, to form the **grammatical predicate.** (See Uses of the Verb *Be*, page 19.)

The **simple** or **grammatical predicate** is the *verb*, or the *verb* and the *attribute* taken *alone*.

The **complex** or **logical predicate** is the simple predicate taken with its modifiers.

Ex.—The redbreast *loves to build and warble there.*—GRAY.

In this sentence *loves*, is the *simple predicate;* and *loves to build and warble there*, is the *complex* or *logical predicate.*

A *finite* verb must be used in the predicate, as neither the *infinitive* nor the *participle* has the power to make an assertion.

Both the infinitive and the participle may be used, however, as *attributes*.

Ex.—He ***is to be educated*** in Boston.

In this sentence *is*, is the finite verb, used to make the assertion; *to be educated* is the *passive infinitive* of the verb *educate*, used as *attribute*. (See Infinitive used as attribute.)

The ***participle*** is used as a ***verbal*** attribute in the *progressive form* of the verb, and in the *perfect tenses*.

Ex.—The sun ***is rising***. The sun ***has risen***.

ELEMENTS OF THE SENTENCE.

The ***elements*** of a *sentence* are the *words, phrases* or *clauses* of which *it* is composed.

The *elements* of a sentence are divided into:

    1.—***Principal elements.***
    2.—***Subordinate elements.***

The ***principal elements*** are the *subject* and the *predicate*.

The *subject* and the *predicate* are called *principal elements*, because no sentence can be formed without them; and all *subordinate elements* depend upon them.

The ***subordinate elements*** are those which depend upon and modify the *principal elements*.

The *subordinate elements* are:

    1—The ***Adjective element.***
    2.—The ***Objective element.***
    3.—The ***Adverbial element.***

All the elements are found in the following sentence:

And little footsteps lightly print the ground.—GRAY.

ELEMENTS OF THE SENTENCE. 13

The *elements* which enter into the construction of *sentences* are, *in form,—words, phrases,* or *clauses.*

Each of these forms may be used as follows:

1.—*Subject.*
2.—*Predicate.*
3.—*Adjective Element.*
4.—*Objective Element.*
5.—*Adverbial Element.*

Word element—Subject and predicate. *Bells ring*

Phrase element—Subject and predicate. *To be is to exist.*

Clause element, *as subject. That you are mistaken is certain.*

Clause element, *as* predicate nominative. The cause of his leaving was, *that he was disappointed.*

NOTE.—The subordinate elements, also, may take any of these forms.

The *word element is a single word used to express an idea, without the aid of a relation word.* It matters not how many *modifiers* it may have, *it* should be called a *word element.*

The **Phrase element** *is a verb in the infinitive mode, or a preposition and its object.*

Sometimes the *sign* of the infinitive, the particle *to*, is omitted, and sometimes the *preposition* belonging to the phrase is omitted, but in *both cases* the *element* should be called a *phrase element.*

NOTE.—The term *phrase* is usually applied to *any group of words* which does not contain a finite verb ; but, in the *analysis* of *sentences*, the term *phrase* should be restricted to the *forms* spoken of above.

Independent elements are certain words or expressions which have no grammatical relation to *any sentence, or any part of a sentence*, though they usually accompany a sentence.

They are used often in *exclamations*, and in *conversation*.

The principal *independent elements* consist of *expressions* of *emotion;* the most of such are always incomplete:—
>Oh how beautiful!
>Oh! but to breathe the breath
>Of the cowslip and primrose sweet!—HOOD.

The *nominative independent* by *address :—*
>Adam, where art thou!—BIBLE.

The *Adverbs*, now, well, why:
>*Now*, what have you done!
>*Well*, can it be true?
>*Why*, you said so.

And the *Interjections :—*
>Oh! Ah! Alas! What! etc.

Other independent elements will be given hereafter.

Independent elements should be separated from the sentence by a comma.

A word, phrase or clause added to an element to vary its meaning is called a **modifier**.

A *simple element* is one which is not modified.

Ex.—*Boys run.*

A *complex element* is a modified element, or an element taken with its modifier, or modifiers.

Ex.—*Three* boys run *fast*.

The basis of an element is the element which is modified; *boys* is the basis of *three boys;* and *run* is the basis of *run fast.*

A *compound element* is one which consists of two or more similar elements, coördinately united by conjunctions, either expressed or understood.

Ex.—*Apples, peaches* and *pears* are in market now.

Coördinate elements do not modify each other, or one another, but when combined they may modify some other element.

Ex.—*Clear* and *beautiful* skies looked down smilingly upon the landscape.

In this sentence *clear* and *beautiful* are coördinate elements, making a compound adjective element; but subordinate to *skies*, which they modify.

CLASSES OF SENTENCES.

SENTENCES CLASSIFIED BY THEIR USE.

Thought may be *expressed* by means of words, in *four* different *ways;* there are, therefore, *four different kinds of sentences:*

        1.—*Declarative.*
        2.—*Interrogative.*
        3.—*Imperative.*
        4.—*Exclamative.*

A *Declarative sentence* is one that makes an *affirmation* or a *denial.*

Ex.—*The hunters returned yesterday.*
The hunters did not return yesterday.

The hunters may return to-morrow.

If the hunters return to-morrow, they will supply us with game for the feast.

An *Interrogative sentence* is used to ask a question.

Ex.—Have you been to Crystal Lake to-day?
Is it time to go home?

Interrogative sentences are not always used to ask for *information.*

They are sometimes used for *rhetorical effect;* and they are then called *questions of appeal.*

Ex.—Is there not a time appointed unto man to die? There is.
Shall we submit to the oppression of a tyrant? We shall not.

When the question of appeal is *negative*, an affirmative answer is expected; and when it is *affirmative*, a negative answer is expected, as will be seen above.

An *Imperative sentence* is used to express a command, an entreaty, a petition, or a request.

Ex.—Give ear, O my people, to my law.
Maintain the ground where thou standest.

NOTE.—*The relative position of the speaker and the one spoken to decides whether the imperative sentence is a command, an entreaty, a petition, or a request.*

An *Exclamative,* or as it is commonly called, an *exclamatory* sentence, is one used to express some strong emotion of pain, pleasure, astonishment, approbation, disapprobation, etc.

Exclamative sentences are often mere fragments, not admitting of analysis.

Ex.—Impossible!
What a lovely day!
How terrible!

Such expressions are of the nature of the *Interjection*, therefore an exclamation point should be placed after them.

When two or more different kinds are united to form one sentence, it is called a *mixed sentence*.

Ex.—*Tell* me how much money you *want*, and I *will give* it to you.

He *said* to me, *do you know* where the paper is published?

The first one of the sentences consists of an imperative proposition, and a declarative proposition; and the second, of a declarative proposition, and an interrogative proposition. Both are mixed sentences.

SENTENCES CLASSIFIED ACCORDING TO STRUCTURE.

Sentences are classified according to their *structure* into:

    1.—*Simple* sentences.
    2.—*Complex* sentences.
    3.—*Compound* sentences.

A *simple sentence* consists of a single proposition.
Ex.—*Bells ring.*

A simple sentence may consist of two words only, or of an indefinite number of words: for both subject and predicate may take a great many modifiers.

Ex.—It is a glorious land, with snowy, bold, and magnificent mountains; deep, narrow and well wooded valleys:

bleak plateau and slopes; wild ravines; clear and picturesque lakes, immense forests of birch, pine and fir trees.

This sentence is simple, though some of the elements are complex, and some compound.

Sentences of great length are sometimes difficult to comprehend, it is better, therefore, to separate them into short and simple statements.

Brevity often adds beauty and clearness to a statement.

A *complex sentence* consists of at least two propositions, one *principal*, and one *subordinate*.

Ex.—When the tree was cut down, two birds flew in circles above his head.

The complex sentence may contain several subordinate clauses, and may be extended to any length desirable, as in the following:

When the tree was cut down, two birds flew in circles above his head, uttering piercing and mournful cries, because their nest of little fledglings was utterly destroyed.

The parts of a complex sentence are called *clauses;* the *principal clause*, and the *subordinate clause*.

The subordinate clause is joined to the principal clause by a subordinate *connective.*

A *compound sentence* consists of two or more independent propositions connected by coördinate conjunctions.

Ex.—The man cut down the tree, and a nest containing some beautiful little birds was utterly destroyed.

ANALYSIS.

Analysis is the process by which the *whole* is resolved or separated into its *component elements*, or *parts*.

In its application to language, *analysis* refers to a *complete* separation of a sentence into its elements; and a careful examination of *each*, in its reference to the *whole*, or to *some other element*.

Syntax and *Analysis* are so intimately related that they may properly be treated of together.

As it is impossible to analyze a sentence systematically, or with any correctness whatever, if the construction be faulty, it will be necessary to require the pupil to be very careful in preparing original sentences for practical analysis.

Original sentences should be required of the pupil every day.

Sentences properly constructed will separate into their constituent elements with ease, when the laws of analysis are applied.

THE SIMPLE SENTENCE.

THE VERB BE.

The verb *Be* is the life principle of language. Without it, no statement can be made.

Every verb has two distinct *elements*,—one is the *assertive*, the other, the *attributive*.

When the assertive part is separated from the attributive, the latter becomes a participle, having no power whatever to express a thought. The assertive element is the verb *Be*, called the **copula**; it is found in all verbs, though not always expressed.

In the sentence,

Snow is falling,

the copula and the attribute are both expressed; is, is the **copula**, and *falling*, the attribute.

But they are often blended; then a new word is formed in which neither is seen; just as the blending of two colors makes a new one, which resembles neither of the originals. *Is falling* is equivalent to *falls*.

The *new word* is called an *attributive verb*; therefore,

The attributive verb is the one word in which both the copula and the attribute are blended.

Fall, *rise*, *come*, *run*, etc., are attributive verbs.

The verb *Be* has two uses.

1. When used *alone*, it denotes *existence*, as, God *is*, I think, therefore, I *am*, *i. e.*, I *exist*. Thus used, Be is an attributive verb.

Such sentences are often introduced by the word *there*, which is simply a word of *euphony*, forming no material part of the sentence; as *There* is a God.

2. When used to join an attribute to the subject, it is called the *copula*.

As a *copula*, or *link*, it may connect

a substantive attribute;
an adjective attribute;
a verbal attribute.

The adverb cannot be used as an attribute.

Exercises.—

1. A substantive attribute: The canary is a *bird*.

2. An adjective attribute: The canary is *pretty*.
3. A verbal attribute; The canary is *singing*.

MODEL FOR ANALYSIS.

The simplest form of the sentence.

God is.

It is a proposition,—it is a combination of a subject and a predicate.

It is the expression of a thought in words; therefore it is a *sentence*.

It is a *simple sentence*, it contains but one proposition.

God is the subject; it is a word which represents that of which the being, or existence is affirmed.

Is is the predicate; it is a word used to affirm the being or existence of God.

I EXERCISE.

I am. He was. They were. There are joys. There were sorrows. There was pleasure.

The verb Be when used to denote existence is usually followed by an adverbial element of place; as, I am here. He was in town.

Write ten sentences containing the verb Be, used to denote existence.

THE VERB BE USED AS COPULA.

The verb *Be* is always *intransitive*.

It *asserts* no action whatever of the subject, therefore it has no power to govern.

The *noun* or the *pronoun* following it represents the subject in another form, and must agree with it in all that they have in common.

The subject of every *finite verb* must be in the *nomina-*

tive case; and the noun or pronoun connected to it by the verb Be, must be in the nominative case also.

The verb *Be* when used to connect an attribute to the subject is called a copula, or link.

RULE I.

The subject of a finite verb must be in the nominative case.

RULE II.

The noun or pronoun connected to the subject of a finite verb, by the copula, must be in the nominative case.

PRACTICAL.

Such expressions as It is him; It is her; It is them; are incorrect; say, It is I; It is he; It is she; It is they.

MODEL FOR ANALYSIS.

Lilies are Flowers.

It is a proposition; it is the combination of a *subject* and a *predicate*.

It is the expression of a thought in words; therefore it is a sentence.

It is a simple sentence; it contains but one proposition.

Lilies is the subject; it is that of which the attribute, *flowers*, is asserted.

Are flowers is the predicate; it is that which is affirmed of *lilies*.

Are is the copula; it is a form of the verb *Be*, used to connect the substantive attribute *flowers* to the subject *lilies*.

Flowers is the substantive attribute; a word used to represent the class of objects to which the subject belongs. It agrees with the subject in person, number, and gender, and is also in the nominative case to agree with the subject, according to Rule II.

Exercises upon the verb *Be*, used as copula, to connect a substantive attribute.

It is I.	Oranges are fruit.
It is he.	Indians are savages.
It is she.	Diamonds are stones.
It is thou.	Pines are evergreens.
It is you.	Bees are insects.

Write fifteen sentences to illustrate Rule II.

RULE III.

The adjective connected by the copula to the subject must represent some characteristic property of the subject.

PRACTICAL.

Great care should be taken to avoid the use of an adjective in the *predicate*, which represents a *quality* or a *condition* which, from the nature of the subject, could not belong to it.

Careless as well as ignorant speakers often violate Rule III. by using such expressions as,—It *is awful*, It *is splendid*, It *is nice*, when in reality the object represented by *it*, could not, from its nature, possess an element of *awe*, or *splendor*, and the attribute *nice* is predicated of almost every object under the sun, whether small or great.

Teachers should not regard this as a matter of small importance, but should promptly and persistently call the attention of the pupil to his mistake, and aid him in acquiring a correct habit in the use of the predicate adjective.

MODEL FOR ANALYSIS.

Lilies are Beautiful.

It is a proposition; it is a combination of a subject and a predicate.

It is the expression of a thought in words; therefore it is a sentence.

It is a simple sentence; it contains but one proposition.

Lilies is the subject; it is a word which represents that of which the attribute, *beautiful*, is asserted.

Are beautiful is the predicate; it is that which is asserted of the subject.

Are is the copula; it is the form of the verb *Be*, used to connect the adjective attribute, *beautiful*, to the subject, *lilies*.

Beautiful is the adjective attribute, a word used to represent a quality that is natural to the subject, *lilies*, and agrees with it according to Rule III.

EXERCISE I.

The verb *Be* used to connect an adjective attribute to the subject.

Winds were cold.
Snow is white.
Apples are sour.
Job was patient.
Water is clear.

Jewels are valuable.
Thou art merciful.
Mary is careful.
John is faithful.
Fawns are graceful.

Write ten sentences to illustrate Rule III.

RULE IV.

The verbal attribute connected to the subject by the verb *Be*, must represent some action or state natural to the subject.

MODEL FOR ANALYSIS.

Lilies are growing.

It is a proposition; it is the combination of a subject and a predicate.

It is the expression of a thought in words; therefore it is a *sentence*.

It is a simple sentence; it contains but one proposition.

Lilies is the subject; it is that about which the action, *growing*, is affirmed.

Are growing is the predicate; it is that which is asserted of the subject.

Are is the copula; it is a form of the verb *Be* used to connect a verbal attribute to the subject.

Growing is the *verbal attribute*; a word used to represent an action that is natural to the subject, with which it agrees according to Rule IV.

PRACTICAL.

Do not predicate an *action* of the subject which it can not perform, or a *state* which is not natural to it.

Say the lark is *singing*, not the lark is *cooing*; the boy is *lying* on the ground, not, *the boy* is *laying* on the ground, when reference is made to his being prostrate on the ground; he is *sitting* in a chair, not he is *setting* in a chair.

EXERCISE II.

The verb *Be* used to connect a verbal attribute to the subject.

Bells are ringing.
Ships were sailing.
Snow is falling.
Ice is melting.
Boys were skating.
Eagles are screaming.
Doves were cooing.
Thou art sighing.
He is laughing.
Lions were roaring.

The copula is used also to connect to the subject a **passive participle,** which is a verbal attribute used to represent an action received by the subject. The copula and this attribute combined form the passive voice of the verb. The *copula* and the verbal *attribute* should be parsed together as one verb.

Ex.—John is respected.

Note— The infinitive *To Be*, used to connect the **attributive object** of a verb or a preposition to the direct object, will be treated of in connection with the *Double Object*.

Care has been taken to present only the simplest form of the sentence, with no modifiers whatever.

Note.—Some authors, very few, however, have attempted to justify the use of an objective after Be, saying that the construction is a genuine idiom of the English, formed on the analogy of the French *C' est moi*, etc.

The *etc.* remains a mystery to the pupil unacquainted with the French language; but he is impressed with the notion that it contains weighty matter in favor of this usage.

The fact is, that in the French language there are four constructions in which the dative form of the pronoun is used in the place of the nominative form, but the change of form does not change the case of the pronoun.

The nominative singular of the personal pronouns in the French language is:

    First person, *je*, I.
    Second person, *tu*, thou.
    Third person, *il*, he.

But, in the four cases to which reference has been made, *je* becomes *moi*, *tu* becomes *toi*, and *il* becomes *lui*. The plurals change form, also, in the same way.

The four constructions are the following:

1. When the pronoun is used as a substantive attribute, as *c' est moi*, it is I.
2. When the subject is compound, as *lui et moi, nous apprenons le francais*, he and I study French.
3. When used with *plus que* to denote comparison of inequality, as *je suis plus jeune que lui*, I am younger than he.
4. When used to answer questions, as *qui a fait cela?—moi*, who has done that?—I.

If the expression, *it is me*, is a correct translation of *c'est moi*, then him and me are learning French, is a correct translation of *lui et moi nous apprenons le francais ;* I am younger than *him*, is a correct translation of *je suis plus jeune que lui*, and *who has done that? me*, is a correct translation of *qui a fait cela? moi*.

THE SIMPLE SENTENCE. 27

The advocates of this objective form after Be, are careful not to go beyond the first example, including the others under the head of *etc.*

The authors of the French grammars are the highest authority in the matter, and they invariably translate these dative forms into the English, as nominatives.

In some of the grammars, too, the forms, *moi, toi, lui,* etc., are given in the declension of the personal pronouns as second forms of the nominative.—See "Ahn's French Method," page 106.

THE PREPOSITIONAL PHRASE USED AS ATTRIBUTE.

The *prepositional phrase* is often used as attribute, to denote some quality or condition of the subject.

In this use, it is equivalent to an adjective, and, when treated as a whole, should be disposed of as an adjective.

It is a *separable phrase*, however, and each word may be parsed separately.

This construction is somewhat troublesome, from the fact that there are two connectives,—the *copula* and the *preposition.*

Ex.—*He is above reproach.*

According to the best authors, the copula is used to connect the *entire phrase* to the subject, just as it is used to connect a single word.

The preposition, if used as a *relation* word in such construction, which is doubtful, shows the relation of its object to the subject.

In analysis, however, it is better to regard the phrase as inseparable, for such expressions are always weakened by analysis.

This form of the adjective attribute is very common, perhaps because it denotes the property or condition of the subject, with *greater intensity*, and, also, with *more precision* than the adjective.

It is frequently the case that no adjective in the language can be found *to convey the exact meaning* given by the phrase.

In the sentence, *He is above reproach*, the phrase, *above reproach*, has no exact equivalent.

MODEL FOR ANALYSIS.

We are in trouble.

It is a proposition ; it is the combination of a subject and a predicate.

It is the expression of a thought in words, therefore it is a *sentence*.

It is a *simple sentence ;* it contains but one proposition.

We is the subject; it is a word which represents that of which the condition, *in trouble*, is asserted.

Are is the copula; it is a form of the verb *Be*, used to connect the adjective attribute, *in trouble*, to the subject *We*.

In trouble is the adjective attribute; it is a phrase used to represent a condition that is natural to the subject, and agrees with it, according to Rule III.

EXERCISE I.

The Phrase used as Attribute.

He is above reproach.
That is out of the question.
I am in haste.
Mary is at leisure.
He is beneath contempt.

They are in harmony.
John is without friends.
They are in despair.
You are at rest.
James is out of humor.

Write fifteen sentences to illustrate prepositional phrase as attribute.

THE INFINITIVE USED AS ATTRIBUTE.

The infinitive phrase is often used as the attribute of a subject, and forms, with the copula, the grammatical predicate.

When thus used it denotes:
1. Something that ought to be.
    Ex.—*Lessons are to be studied.*
2. An equivalent expression.
    Ex.—*To be is to exist.*
3. What is settled.
    Ex.—*She is to teach.*
4. What is expected.
    Ex.—*He is to return.*
5. What is possible.
    Ex.—*Gold is to be found.*
6. What is required.
    Ex.—*You are to go.*

MODEL FOR ANALYSIS.

Wendell Phillips is to Lecture.

It is a proposition; it is the combination of a subject and a predicate.

It is the expression of a thought in words; therefore it is a *sentence*.

It contains but one proposition; therefore it is a *simple sentence*.

Wendell Phillips is the subject; it is that about which *to lecture* is affirmed.

Is is the copula; a form of the verb *Be*, used to connect the attribute, *to lecture*, to the subject.

To lecture is an infinitive, used as attribute, to denote

something that is expected of the subject, and it belongs to the subject.

In this use, standard authors call the infinitive a substantive attribute; but, like the infinitive in all its uses, it retains the verbal signification, and may be modified as a verb.

EXERCISE II.

The Infinite used as Attribute.

Parents are to be honored.	To obey is to enjoy.
To exterminate is to destroy.	Teachers are to be respected.
I am to go.	Rulers are to be obeyed.
Pearls are to be found.	The house is to rent.
Horses were to be sold.	He is to preach.
Violets are to be seen.	Mary is to sing.

What the infinitive denotes, cannot always be determined upon, easily, without joining to it some adverbial modifier. In the sentence, *Pearls are to be found*, the infinitive is used to denote something possible, as, Pearls are to be found, sometimes, in the rivers.

THE COPULATIVE VERB.

RULE V.

The attribute of a proposition, whether substantive, adjective, or verbal, must agree with the subject when joined to it by a copulative verb.

A verb of complete predication is one which, in itself, indicates, clearly, what it asserts of the subject.

In the sentence, *God is*, it requires no effort of the mind to understand that the fact of the *existence* of the subject is meant.

In the sentence, *John sleeps*, the verb conveys to the mind the state of the subject; and in the following : *he goes, he runs, he writes*, etc , the peculiar kind of action asserted of the subject, by the verb in each sentence, is definitely expressed.

But it has been already shown that the verb *Be*, when it is not used to denote existence, *requires the help of another word, to enable it to make sense*, and that it then performs the office of a copula, or link, to join the *attribute* to the *subject*.

It is, in reality, the *copula proper;* but there are other verbs that resemble it in this respect; therefore they are called *copulative verbs*.

The greater number of these, however, are in their common use, verbs of full, or complete predication ; and it is only in a peculiar use that they join an attribute to the subject.

In the sentence, *he seems*, the verb taken alone means nothing ; but, in *he seems a beggar, he seems sick, he seems determined,* the *added word*, in each case, completes the predication.

The infinitive form of *Be* is usually understood after *become, seem*, and *others*.

Ex.—He seems (to be) determined.

After the passive form of some verbs, the participle *being*, with *as*, is understood.

Ex.—*She is regarded (as being) a good teacher*.

The conjunction, *as*, is, sometimes placed before the attribute, without *being*, when the verb is passive, simply to express the idea of capacity or office, and, perhaps, to give emphasis in some cases.

Ex.—*He was regarded as a good teacher*.

It is said by the best authors that almost any verb may

be used to predicate an attribute of the subject, but the following are those commonly used for this purpose:

become	go,	die,
seem,	get,	continue,
appear,	grow,	come,
look,	bake,	make,
feel,	walk,	taste,
turn,	live,	smell.
remain,		

And the passive form of:

account,	consider,	create,
deem,	regard,	elect,
style,	name,	hear,
call,	think,	paint,
reckon,	say,	appoint.

The *last named*, take after them in the active voice, a *direct object*, and predicate of it an *attributive object*. This construction will be treated of hereafter.

MODEL FOR ANALYSIS.

Bread is baked brown.

It is a proposition; it is a combination of a subject and and a predicate.

It is the expression of a thought in words; therefore it is a *sentence*.

It is a *simple sentence;* it contains but one proposition.

Bread is the subject; it is a word which represents that of which the attribute, *brown*, is asserted.

Is baked brown is the predicate; it is that which is asserted of the subject.

Is baked is the copulative verb, used to connect the

adjective attribute, *brown*, to the subject, *bread*, according to Rule IV.

In this sentence, the adjective *brown* is a second attribute, and represents a quality of the subject, acquired through the action indicated by the verb *baked*.

In all passive forms of the copulative verb, the passive participle used with the verb *Be*, is considered the first attribute, and the noun, adjective, or participle following, the second attribute.

Ex.—*He was called a martyr.* *Called* is the first, or verbal, attribute, and *martyr* the second, or substantive attribute.

PRACTICAL.

It is of great importance that young persons be taught the nature and use of the copulative verb; many, whose attention has not been directed *persistently* to those things, imagine they are using the very best English when they say, *She looks beautifully, I feel miserably, I feel badly*, etc.

One can easily decide when to use an adverb, and when an adjective, by observing the following:

If reference is made to a *quality*, a *property* or a *condition* of the subject, an *adjective*, or an *adjective expression*, should be used after the verb.

But, if the *manner* of the action is referred to, an *adverb* is required.

She looks beautiful; she writes beautifully.

He looks cold, for he has been on the ice; his mother looks coldly on him, because he has disobeyed her.

I feel *bad*, when I am not well, or when I am in trouble; I feel *badly*, when the *sense of touch* is not acute.

C

EXERCISE.

The copulative verb used to connect an attribute to the subject.

It becomes tiresome.
She seems sick.
Leaves turn yellow.
You look cold.
He looks bad.
I feel warm.
I feel miserable.
They remain silent.
Apples get ripe.
It is said to be true.

He is going mad.
She walks a queen.
They stand defenders.
She moves a goddess.
He was called John.
I feel happy.
Henry was made sick.
He was made worse.
He grows desperate.
He was made consul.

Pierce was elected president.
The bread was baked brown.
Stephen died a martyr.
The house is painted white.
He was heard to speak.

Write fifteen sentences to illustrate the rule.

MODIFIERS OF THE SUBJECT.

RULE I.—ANALYSIS.

Any word, whether it be an adjective, a noun, or a pronoun, when joined to the subject to limit or qualify it, must be called in analysis an **adjective element.**

A sentence, in its *simplest* form, is composed of a noun used as the subject, and a finite verb used to assert something of the subject.

In order to convey a thought, with all its shades of meaning, however, it is necessary, in most sentences, to introduce other words for the purpose of modifying both the subject, and the predicate verb.

In the sentence, *birds flew*, the *class* to which the subject, *birds*, belongs is understood at once; and the kind of *action* indicated by the verb, *flew*, is, also, clearly understood; but, still the thought is very indefinite.

Three young white birds flew *from the tree.*

Here the words joined to the subject show the *kind*, the *age*, and the *number* of birds, and the modifier of the predicate shows the *place* where the action was performed.

Thus it is seen that the use of these additional words or phrases will enable a speaker or a writer to make a clear and definite statement, and to extend the simple sentence to any desired length.

The English language is rich in modifying words, yet all those that are used to vary the meaning of the subject, or a noun in any construction, may be classed under four heads:

1. *Limiting adjectives,* which simply restrict the meaning of the noun, without showing any quality or property, whatever, as:

an orange,
two apples,
that man.

2. *Qualifying adjectives,* which show some property or quality natural to the object represented by the noun, as:

a *sweet* orange,
a *sour* apple,
a *wise* man.

3. Nouns or pronouns used to explain or to identify another noun or pronoun, as:

Victoria, *Queen* of England,
Charles, the *boy* of whom I spoke.

4. Nouns or pronouns used to denote *possession*, as:
Mary's book,
his hand.

The adjectives which are used simply to limit the meaning of a noun without designating any quality, include:

1. Articles.
2. Pronominal Adjectives.
3. Numeral Adjectives.

There are *two articles;* the *indefinite* article, *an* or *a*, and the *definite* article, *the*.

The indefinite article *an* is derived from the Anglo-Saxon *ane*, meaning *one;* but there is a shade of difference; *an* is not so exact as *one*, nor is it so emphatic. *An apple*—not *an orange; one apple*—not *two apples*.

It is a mistake to say that *a* becomes *an* before a *vowel* sound; the *change* is made from *an* to *a*.

The changes were made for the sake of *euphony*. First, the *e* was dropped entirely from *ane*, leaving *an;* and afterwards the *n* was dropped from *an*, leaving the *a* only, before words beginning with a *consonant* sound.

It is now regarded as an absolute law of our language, than *an* should be used before words beginning with a *vowel sound*, and *a* before words beginning with a *consonant sound*.

In old English, the form *a* or *o* is found for *an*, even when used as a numeral. We still say, they are both of *a size, i. e.*, both of *one size*.—MASON.

There is a peculiar construction of *an* or *a* with *many, such, what*, and some other words, as, *many a man, such an hour, what a boy*, etc.

In such combinations, *the adjective and the article should be parsed as one word, and should be so considered in analysis.*

Many, followed by *an* or *a,* always limits a noun in the singular, though it at the same time indicates plurality; and the pronoun relating to the singular noun is usually put in the plural; as:

I have heard many an act of devotion, in my life, had Heaven vouchsafed me grace to profit by *them.*

The definite article the is used to point out the particular thing or things spoken of.

It is derived from the Anglo-Saxon *thaet,* which was changed to *that,* and finally, to *the,* but both are used.

There is a *shade* of difference in meaning, however. *That* is the stronger word, and may be used to represent a noun; *the* is not so *emphatic,* and cannot take the place of a noun.

The is sometimes used with a noun taken in its widest sense for a whole race or species; as:

The lion is king of beasts.
The eagle is a noble bird.
Go to the ant, thou sluggard.
The oak is a tall tree.
The violet grows in shady places.

But some nouns are used *in their widest sense,* when *no article* is placed before them. *The* man, always means *one* man;—*man,* used without the article, always refers to the race, as:

Man (all human beings) is endowed with reason.

The noun designating the *profession, trade,* or *occupation* of man, however, when used with *the,* is often taken in its *widest* sense, as:

The physician heals the sick.
The farmer cultivates the soil.

Pronominal Adjectives.

Certain *limiting* adjectives are called **Pronominal Adjectives,** because they may be used, with equal propriety, either as a pronoun, representing a noun understood, or as an adjective, limiting the noun expressed.

When used to represent a *noun understood*, only a few of them require the use of the article, as:

The former, the latter, the same.

Every and *no* require a noun, as neither of them can be used alone to represent a noun.

Pronominal Adjectives are divided into four classes:

1. **Distributives,** or those which refer to things taken singly.

They are *each, every, either, neither.*

2. **Demonstratives,** or those that refer to things, pointing them out definitely, as:

This, that, these, those, former, latter, same.

3. **Reciprocals,** or those which bear a mutual relation.

They are *each other* and *one another.*

4. The **Indefinites,** or those which refer to objects indefinitely. Words of this class are numerous, but the following are the principal:

Some, such, all, none, any, whole, one, other, another.

One and *other* may be declined.

One is not derived from the Anglo-Saxon *ane*, from which the numeral one is derived. It comes from the French *on*, which is an *indefinite pronoun*, derived from the word *homme*, meaning *man*. *On* may be translated as, *anybody, somebody, they, it,* etc., as:

On dit—they say, it is said somebody says, etc.

THE SIMPLE SENTENCE.

PRACTICAL.

Use *either* and *neither* when reference is made to *two things only*, as:
Either of the two books.
Any of the three books.

Do not say, *the two boys help one another*, but, the two boys help *each other*. *One another* should be used with reference to *three* or more persons or things; *each other*, with reference to *two*, only.

This and *these* refer to things near to us, or to something just mentioned; *that* and *those*, to something more distant, or something spoken of before.

THE NUMERAL ADJECTIVES.

Numeral adjectives are those used in *counting*, in *numbering*, and in *multiplying*, as:
One, two, first, threefold.

Those used in counting are called **cardinals**, because they are the *principal, or most important*, as:
One, two, three, twenty, thirty, hundred.

NOTE.—The *cardinal points of the compass* are *the principal points*. Cardinal *red*,—the color worn by the *cardinals*, or *principal* officers of the Catholic Church.

Those used in *numbering* are called **ordinals**, because they point out which thing, or which things, in a series, as:
First, second, ninth, twentieth.

The greater number of the ordinals are derived from the cardinals, and are formed by adding *th*, as:
Sixth, seventh, tenth, hundredth;
but the ordinals corresponding to one, two, three, are:
First, second, third.

Those used to denote *repetition*, or to show how *many times*, are called *multiplicatives*, as:

Once, twice, thrice (these are often used as adverbs), *two-fold, ten-fold, hundred-fold, double, triple, quadruple.*

The numeral adjectives, when used without the noun, yet referring to the noun, either just mentioned or clearly understood, should be parsed as a noun, as:

Where are my books?

Ans. *Two* are on the table, and *three* are in the library. In this sentence *two* and *three* should be parsed as nouns.

When the ordinals are used as nouns, the article is required before them, as:

The first entered; *the second* remained outside.

The *ordinal adjectives* are more definite than the cardinals, as:

Study *one* lesson, *i. e.*, any lesson.

Study the *second* lesson, *i. e.*, a particular lesson.

PRACTICAL.

The numeral adjectives which denote *how many*, must agree in *number* with the noun which they limit, as:

Two boys, *three* miles, *four* feet.

Nouns used with numeral adjectives to denote degrees of *measurement*, should be in the *singular* or in the *plural*, as the case may be, as:

Cut off *one inch* or *two inches* of the string.

Cut off *one foot* or *two feet* of the pole.

Cut off *one yard* or *two yards* of the cloth.

But, when the words *inch, foot, yard*, etc., are used with a numeral adjective, forming a *complex adjective* term, they should always be in the singular, as:

Cut off *two inches* of the *nine-inch* string.

Cut off *three feet* of the *ten-foot* pole.

Cut off *four yards* of the *forty-yard* bolt of cloth.

He surveyed *ten acres* on the east side of the *forty-acre* tract.

Sometimes a *numeral adjective* and a noun combined are used to denote *quantity* or amount. In such cases the verb should always be singular, though the noun be in the plural, as:

Two hundred dollars is all I need.

Ten minutes was all the time allowed me.

But, in speaking of coins, the plural verb should be used, as:

Two hundred *gold dollars* were in the box.

Under this head may be classed such expressions as:

Twice four is eight, five times six is thirty, etc.,

but while the weight of authority is in favor of the use of the singular verb, in the last-named, some good writers use the plural.

QUALIFYING ADJECTIVES.

Adjectives that are joined to nouns to limit them by denoting some *quality*, *property*, or *peculiarity*, are classed under the head of **Qualifying Adjectives**, as:

A *bright* star, a *daily* visit, an *earnest* student.

The greater number of these adjectives are varied to denote different degrees of quality, but there are some that will not admit of comparison. Among the last named are:

1. Those of *absolute* signification, or such as indicate a quality, which, from its nature, can not exist in the object in a greater or a less degree, as:

Mortal, immortal, eternal, everlasting, infinite, almighty, omniscient, etc.

2. Those denoting position, form and material, as:

Vertical, square, woolen, etc.

3. Those derived from proper names, as:

2*

American, Washingtonian.

The words *full, round,* and *perfect,* seem to have an absolute signification, yet some good writers use them in the comparative and the superlative.

☞ Some adjectives, mostly compounds of *a,* can be used only in the predicate, as:

Asleep, alive, awake.

Many of the *qualifying adjectives* may be used in the place of a noun, and parsed as such, when the reference to the noun is clear, but the article must be used with them, as:

The *sweet apples* are in the basket, but the *sour* are in the box.

NOTE.—Some authors say that in expressions such as the above, the adjectives are not used as nouns, but should be parsed as adjectives limiting a noun understood; and, that, in such as the following: "The *poor* ye have always with you," the adjective should be parsed as a noun. It would seem, however, that the distinction is too nice to be noticed, if there be really any distinction whatever.

The *adjective,* as it has already been explained, is used to limit *nouns only,* but there is a peculiar, though a very common construction, in which the adjective limits a complex idea, formed by a noun and an adjective combined, as:

I saw *beautiful* American silk.

She had a *large* white rose.

In the first sentence, *beautiful* modifies *American silk,* and in the second sentence, *large* modifies *white rose.*

A careful distinction should be made between the *adjective element,* which is *always* a modifier, and the *adjective attribute,* which is *never* a modifier.

To *modify* is to vary, to give a new form to, and to change, not only the *form* of the word itself, but also to change the *meaning,* to a certain extent.

A change in the *word itself* is a modification of the word, as, from the singular to the plural.

Ex.—*Man, men ; boy, boys.*

Changes are made also by additional words, and these words are called *modifiers*. They are always *subordinate* words depending upon the subject, or any noun which they are used to modify, as:

A *rich* man; a *good* boy.

But, to *predicate* is *to affirm, to assert, to declare,* or *to state some attribute of the subject.*

The adjective, therefore, used with the copula, or with the copulative verb, to form the *grammatical predicate,* is simply the word used as the name of a quality which is declared to exist in the subject, and for that reason it is said to belong to the subject.

The grammatical subject and the grammatical predicate are both *principal elements,* therefore as the adjective attributive forms a part of the grammatical predicate, it can not be a modifier; for all modifiers, as it has been said, are *subordinate elements.*

PARTICIPLES.

Participles, when used as modifiers of the noun, are included under the head of *qualifying adjectives.*

But, as they differ materially from the qualifying adjective proper, it is thought necessary to explain, carefully, their nature as well as their uses.

A participle is not a distinct part of speech. It is a word which partakes of the nature of a verb, and of some other part of speech, as the name indicates; for the word *participle* is derived from the Latin word *participare,* meaning *to partake.*

The participle is derived from a verb, and in all its uses retains the *signification of a verb,* but it can not be used to *assert.*

In the construction of a sentence it is used as an *adjective* or a *noun*, seldom, if ever, as an *adverb*.

It has been stated that every verb has two parts, the *assertive part* or *copula*, and the *attributive part*.

When the verb is deprived of the power of asserting, the *attributive* part alone is left, and this part is called a *participle*.

As the participle always retains the signification of the verb from which it is derived, it follows:

1. That if the verb is an *active transitive* verb, its *participles* must be *active* and *transitive*, as:

John loved his mother.

Here *loved* is an active transitive verb, and governs the object, *mother;* and in the expression, *John loving his mother*, the participle *loving* retains the active transitive signification of the verb *love*, from which it is derived, and it also governs the object, *mother*.

In the expression, *John loved by his mother*, the participle, though *passive* in form, still retains the *active transitive signification* of the verb *love*, for:

Neither a verb nor a participle can take a passive form (except in certain idioms, as: he *is come*, they *are gone*, etc.) if it has not an active transitive signification.

When a verb is *transitive*, it asserts an action which passes from the *actor*, and produces an effect upon some *object* or *objects*.

The *subject* of a verb does not *necessarily* represent an actor, but it, as often, perhaps, represents a *person or a thing acted upon;* therefore, it is the *subject* in such sentences that is in fact, *passive;* and it follows:

Though the nature of the verb is not changed, it takes what is called a passive form, only to show that the subject, instead of acting, is the receiver of the act.

As the *participle* must retain the nature of the verb from which it is derived, the *passive participle* must retain an active transitive signification, and is used, *not to assert, but simply to denote the reception of an act by the subject, or a noun in other constructions.*

2. If the *verb* from which the participle is derived is an *active intransitive verb*, the participle is an *active intransitive participle*, as:

The sun *rises;*

here *rises* is an active intransitive verb; and in the expression, *the sun rising*, the participle is active and intransitive.

3. If the verb expresses *being*, the participle will denote *being*, as:

Mary *is* here. Mary *being* here.

4. If the verb asserts *state*, the participle denotes *state*, as:

The child *sleeps* on the ground. The child *sleeping* on the ground.

NOTE.—The participle is often used as a noun, and, sometimes, also, seems to have an adverbial signification, but in this lesson it will be treated of only in its use as a modifier of the subject, or of nouns in other constructions in the simple sentence, as:

The singing bird; the twinkling star; a cultivated field; a refined manner.

In the above expressions, the participles are used to limit the nouns, and are placed before the nouns.

These are called *participial adjectives.*

The participle in an *abridged proposition* introduces an *adjective* element, which is called *participial construction;* but, though this participle introduces and forms a part of the adjective element, it should not be called a *participial adjective.*

NOTE.—Careful instruction should be given in the method of parsing a participial adjective.

Note.—A celebrated author says: *When a participle is so used (before the noun) call it a participial adjective and parse it as any other adjective;* but, it would seem better to instruct the pupil in all that pertains to the participle, excepting those points which are beyond his comprehension.

The pupil in the common schools cannot understand, easily, references made to the Latin; therefore it is thought better to omit any discussion on the *gerund* or the *gerundive.*

But the pupil can understand, with little effort, that the word *singing,* in the sentence, *the singing bird is in the* cage, though it is used to modify the word *bird,* differs materially from the word *beautiful,* in the sentence, " the *beautiful* bird is in the cage."

This difference is not a difference in use; for both words are used for the same purpose, *i. e.,* to modify a noun; but the words themselves differ.

The word *beautiful,* as well as the other qualifying adjectives, is always, and in every construction, used to qualify a noun, even though the noun be understood.

The word *singing,* however (and all the present active participles) may be used in six different constructions; yet it never loses the nature of the verb from which it is derived; in all these constructions it retains the idea of action.

Illustration.—A piece of stone may be made the size, the shape, and the color of a brick; and it may be used in the construction of a house, as a brick is used; yet it will not lose one element of its nature—*it will still be stone.*

Note.—The passive participles have four different constructions; the perfect active and the perfect passive participles have, each, two different constructions. These will be explained hereafter.

Great care should be taken to instruct pupils in the correct use of the participle.

Habit is more powerful in controlling speech than knowledge is; therefore, in many cases, the teacher will find constant and persistent efforts necessary on his part to aid his pupils in freeing themselves from the habit of using such expressions as:

1. I seen it. You done it.

These are incorrect, because both *seen* and *done* are participles; and no participle, when used alone, has any power to make an assertion. Say:

I saw it. You did it.

2. I have saw. I have went. The bell has rang.

These expressions are incorrect, because the words *saw*, *went*, and *rang* are verbs, in the past tense; and the last word of every verb in the perfect tense must be a *participle*. Say:

I have seen. I have gone. The bell has rung.

The participle when used with any auxiliary verb is parsed with the auxiliary, the two forming one verb.

3. I had ought to go.

This expression is not only inelegant, but there is not the shadow of an argument in favor of its use. The verb *ought* is a defective verb; it has no participle, therefore it can not have a perfect tense. Say:

I ought to go.

MODEL.

He surveyed ten acres of the forty-acre tract.

This is a sentence, it is the expression of a thought in words.

It is a simple sentence, it contains but one proposition

Declarative it makes an affirmation.

He is the subject, unmodified.

Surveyed is the simple predicate, it is modified by *ten acres of the forty-acre tract*, a complex objective word element. *Acres* is the basis, modified by *ten*, a simple adjective element, and by *of the forty-acre tract*, a complex adjective element, tract is modified by *forty-acre*, a complex adjective element, an inseparable adjective term.

MODIFICATION OF THE SUBJECT.—APPOSITION.

RULE II.—ANALYSIS.

A noun or a personal pronoun in apposition with another noun or pronoun, must be in the same case; and, in analysis, it should be called an adjective element.

Apposition is from the Latin **Appositus**, which means *put to;* the noun in apposition is *put to* the other noun, or by the side of it.

Abraham, the servant of the Lord.

Hope, the charmer.

Apposition proper, does not include the *predicate nominative*, as some have supposed; for:

1. The predicate nominative is not *put to* nor by the side of the subject.

2. The noun or pronoun in apposition with the subject is used as a modifier of the subject, and thus becomes, itself, a part of the logical, or complex subject.

As it must be in the same construction as the subject, it can not possibly form a part of the predicate; but the Attribute, or predicate nominative forms a *material part* of the grammatical predicate.

The *noun* or the *personal pronoun*, however, may be

used in apposition with a noun or a pronoun in any construction, as:

1. Apposition with the subject nominative:
Snow-Bound, a beautiful *poem*, was written by Whittier.

2. Apposition with the predicate nominative:
This is *Snow-Bound*, a beautiful *poem* written by Whittier.

3. Apposition with the objective:
I am reading *Snow-Bound*, a beautiful *poem* by Whittier.

4. Apposition with the possessive:
Whittier the *poet's* Snow-Bound is a beautiful poem.

5. Apposition with the nominative independent:
O *sun, source* of all light!

In the fourth illustration the word *Whittier* is the real possessive, and the word *poet* is in the *possessive only* to agree with Whittier, but the best writers place the sign of possession with the last word only.

In the construction of sentences, apposition has several different uses, all of them important, as:

1. To identify—
Your friend, *Mr. Brown*, called this morning.

2. To describe—
O my coevals, *remnants* of yourselves!"

3. To explain—
Tired nature's sweet *restorer*, balmy *sleep*.

4. In repetitions for the sake of emphasis—
A traitor, a *traitor* to his country.

The connectives, *namely, as, to-wit,* and others are sometimes used to make the noun in apposition emphatic, as:

You, *as* my guardian, have a right to object.

POSSESSIVES.

RULE III.—ANALYSIS.

A noun or a pronoun used to limit a noun in any construction, by denoting possession, must, in analysis, be called an adjective element.

A noun or a pronoun may be used to denote:
1. Ownership, as:
John's horse; *my* book.
2. Source or origin, as:
The *North's* cold winter blasts; the *South's* warm gentle zephyrs.
3. Fitness of adaptation, as:
Men's hats; *children's* shoes.
4. The relation of a part to the whole, as:
The *river's* source; *Mary's* hand.
5. Kindred or social relations, as:
His friend; *your* enemy; *my* father.
6. Result of some action upon, as:
Stephen's martyrdom.
7. Relation of time, place, measurement and weight, as:
A *day's* work; *America's* mountains; a *yard's* length; a *pound's* weight.

The possessive relations are often expressed by the preposition and its object, as:
The house *of my father.*
The cold winter blasts *from the* North.
Shoes *for children.*
The source *of the river.*

There is a *figurative* use of the possessive in some compound words —names of plants; these words should always be written with the sign of possession, and should always be parsed as one word, as:

Wolf's-bane, lamb's-tongue, Job's-tears, etc.

It is necessary to observe the difference between these words and others which resemble them, but, though they suggest the idea of possession, they do not take the possessive sign, as:

Ratsbane; herdsman.

The last mentioned are taken in their literal signification, and are written without the sign of possession.

The word *wolf's-bane* is the name of a plant; it is used figuratively; but the word *rats-bane* is the name of a poison; and it is used, as it has been said, in its literal meaning.

PRACTICAL.

The *pronouns* in the possessive case do not take the *apostrophe*, but they have a peculiar form, as:

The child hurt *its* (not it's) hand.

COMPLEX POSSESSIVES.

There are certain combinations of words which form a complex possessive.

These combinations should be considered inseparable in analysis; the last word takes the sign of possession, as:

The jewels in the *Queen of England's* crown are beautiful and rare.

But when possession is predicated, the first noun in the group of words takes the sign, as:

"There shall nothing die of all that is the *children's* of Israel."—*Exodus* ix. 4.

COMPOUND POSSESSIVES.

When several nouns in the possessive are coördinate in construction, each limiting one common object, the last word only, takes the sign, as:

Taylor, Berry and Brown's store; that is, *one* store.

William and Mary's reign; that is, *one* reign.

But, when the *coördinate* terms in the possessive do not limit the noun by denoting *joint* ownership or possession, each word should take the sign, as:

Greene's, Mason's, and Butler's Grammar; that is, *three* grammars.

POSSESSIVES.

There is a peculiar construction in which a noun in the possessive case is modified by a noun or a pronoun in the possessive, as:

John's brother's knife; His friend's house.

In the sentence above, the *two* possessives combined, form *one complex adjective element,* used to limit the noun.

Sometimes an *adjective* is used to limit a noun in the possessive, thus forming a complex adjective element, as:

The Ancient Mariner's Agony.

In the above sentence *Agony* is modified by *Ancient Mariner's,* a complex adjective element.

This kind of modification must be carefully distinguished from the modification of a complex idea, formed by the combination of a noun and an adjective.

This combination is explained on Page 42.

The difference may be easily shown by omitting the word next to the noun; thus in the expression,

Ancient historical records,

if the word *historical* were omitted, the word *ancient* would still limit the word records.

In the sentence given above, however, *The Ancient Mariner's Agony*, if the word *Mariner's* were omitted, *Ancient* would not modify *Agony*.

Also, in the expression, *Mary's teacher's library*, *Mary* does not modify *teacher's library*, but the word *teacher* only.

If the word *teacher's* be omitted, it will be seen, at once, that by making *Mary* a modifier of *library*, the meaning is entirely changed.

MODELS FOR ANALYSIS.—I.

Every wise man is prudent.

This is a proposition; it is the combination of a subject and a predicate.

It is the expression of a thought in words; therefore it is a *sentence*.

It is a *simple sentence*; it contains but one proposition.

It is a declarative sentence; it makes an affirmation.

Man is the subject; it is that about something which is said.

Is prudent is the predicate; it is what is said of the subject.

The subject *Man* is limited by the adjective element *wise*, and the complex idea *wise man* is limited by *every*, an adjective element.

The predicate is formed of the copula *is* and the adjective attribute *prudent*.

The predicate is not limited.

Any element which is limited in any way is called a complex element.

NOTE.—When the subject is not limited, it is called the *simple* or *grammatical subject*.

When it is limited, it is called the *complex* or *logical subject*.

MODEL II.

His brother's knife is broken.

This is a proposition; it is the combination of a subject and a predicate.

It is the expression of a thought in words; therefore it is a sentence.

It is a *simple sentence*; it contains but one proposition.

Knife is the simple subject.

His brother's knife is the complex subject.

Is broken is the predicate.

The simple subject *knife* is limited by the complex adjective element, *his brother's;* the basis of which is *brother's*, limited by the adjective attribute *his*.

The predicate is composed of the copula *is* and the attribute *broken*.

It is not limited.

MODEL III.

Venus, the evening star, is brilliant.

This is a proposition; it is the combination of a subject and a predicate.

It is a *sentence;* it is the expression of a thought in in words.

It is *simple sentence;* it contains but one proposition.

Declarative, it asserts or declares something.

Venus is the simple subject.

Venus, the evening star, is the complex subject.

Is brilliant is the predicate.

The simple subject, *Venus*, is modified by the complex adjective element, *the evening star;* the basis of which is *star*, a noun in apposition with *Venus*. Star is modified by *evening*, an adjective element; and the complex idea, *evening star*, is modified by the adjective element *the*.

Is brilliant, the predicate, is composed of the copula *is* and the adjective attribute *brilliant*. It is not modified.

The subject may be limited also, by a compound adjective element, as:

A wise and good man should be our ruler.

When the conjunction is omitted, a comma should be placed between the two adjective elements.

In the sentence above, *wise* and *good* are elements of equal rank, each depending upon and modifying the subject *man*.

RULE IV.—ANALYSIS.

A preposition and its object, or an infinitive may be used to limit the meaning of a noun, and in analysis should be called an **adjective word** *element*.

A *phrase*, in its broadest sense, is any group of words which does not contain a *finite verb*, as:

A very large river.

But, in the analysis of sentences, the term *phrase* will be applied to the *infinitive*, and the *preposition and its object* only, as:

At home, in town, to go, to sing.

The prepositional phrase is often used as an *adjective element;* and the relation is usually shown by *of*, as:

A thing *of beauty;* An hour *of happiness;* The top *of the tree*.

Any preposition, however, may be used to show the relation of its object to a noun, as:

The birds *in the cage* are beautiful.
The tree *by* the fountain is an oak.
The boy *in* the house is my brother.
The girl *at* the window is your sister.

The stars *above* us are brilliant.

Each phrase in the above sentences is an adjective element.

This may be proved by expanding the phrase into an adjective clause, as:

The tree *by* the fountain,—the tree *which is by* the fountain.

The girl *at* the window,—the girl *who is at* the window, etc.

These prepositional phrases, when used in the clauses, are *adverbial elements;* but when the clauses are abridged, whatever part of the element remains, takes, not only the character, but the name. also, of the clause of which it once formed a part.

MODEL FOR ANALYSIS.

The time to return was set.

It is a proposition; it is the combination of a subject and a predicate.

It is the expression of a thought in words; therefore it is a sentence.

It is a simple sentence; it contains but one proposition.

Time is the simple subject.

The time to return is the complex subject.

Was set is the predicate.

Time, the simple subject, is modified by *the,* a simple adjective element.

It is also modified by *to return,* an infinitive used as an adjective element.

The predicate is composed of the copula *is,* and the verbal attribute *set.* It is not modified.

EXERCISES.

The *two* good boys are studying.

Three weary pilgrims are resting.
Singing birds were sold.
The sun, a snow-blown traveler, sank, etc.—WHITTIER.
The hour *of rest* has come.
Houses *to rent* are scarce.

> "Lives the Arrow-maker's daughter,
> Minnehaha, Laughing Water,
> Handsomest of all the women."—*Longfellow.*

OBJECTIVE ELEMENT.

RULE V.—ANALYSIS.

Any word used to complete the meaning of a transitive verb, or its participles, is in the objective case; and in analysis should be called an objective word element.

A *transitive verb* is one which shows that the action passes from the subject, either a person or a thing, and terminates with some other person or thing, affecting it in some way indicated by the verb; as:

He *cut* the *apple.*
Mary *loves* her *mother.*

The subject of the verb may be the *actor;* or it may be the *receiver of the act;* but, in either case, the verb is *transitive,* as:

The boy *killed* the *bird.*

In this sentence *killed* is a *transitive* verb, in the *active voice,* and is used to assert the kind of action performed by the subject.

But, in the sentence, The bird *was killed* by the boy, *was killed* is a *transitive* verb, in the *passive voice,* and is used to assert the kind of action *received* by the subject.

In analysis, the object upon which the action terminates, should be called the *direct* objective element.

MODEL FOR ANALYSIS.

I broke the pitcher myself.

It is a proposition; it is the combination of a subject and a predicate.

It is the expression of a thought in words; therefore it is a sentence.

It is a simple sentence; it contains but one proposition.

I is the subject; it is a word which represents the person of whom the action indicated by the verb *broke* is asserted. It is modified by *myself*, an adjective element, by apposition, used for the sake of emphasis.

Broke, the simple predicate, is modified by the complex direct objective element, *the pitcher*, the basis of which is *pitcher*, modified by the adjective element *the*.

Some verbs are always transitive, as:

Eat, write, teach, see, love, destroy, read, etc.

They require an object to complete their meaning; and always suggest an object, if one is not expressed.

When one says, *I read every night*, there is no doubt whatever in the mind of the hearer,—he knows that the *action* indicated by the word *read*, terminates on some object; if one eats, he must exert an action upon something; and the verb *teach* always suggests two parties,—*a subject and an object.*

NOTE.—*Authors* who assert that a *verb* should be called *transitive, only* when an *object* is expressed, are, probably, *not aware* of the *confusion* and *uncertainty* produced in the minds of *teachers* and *pupils*, by such a *statement*.

Some verbs properly classed with *transitive* verbs, when used in a *peculiar* signification, become *intransitive*, as:

Gather, break, sweep, move, melt, and others.

THE SIMPLE SENTENCE.

Transitive.	*Intransitive.*
He gathers *nuts*.	The clouds *gather*.
She breaks the *glass*.	The day *breaks*.
I swept the *floor*.	The wind *swept by*.
John melted the *lead*.	The ice *melts*.
He moved the *chair*.	She *moved* gracefully.

In the *sentences* above, under the *head* of *Intransitive*, no *object* is suggested by the *verbs;* yet, when these *verbs* are spoken of *alone* (when not in a sentence) they should be called *transitive*, for they are *commonly so used*; one may *gather, break, sweep, melt,* and *move* a great many things.

An *intransitive* verb is one which represents an *action* that does *not* pass from the *subject*, but expresses, *in full*, the *idea* intended to be conveyed, without even *suggesting* an object, as:

Rise, fall, go, come, lie (to recline), *sit,* etc.

Such verbs are *always* intransitive.

The verbs *be, become,* and *seem,* also, are always intransitive.

Some *intransitive* verbs become *transitive* by a peculiar use.

1. When *followed* by a *noun* of *kindred signification*, as:
    He *lived* a happy *life*.
    He *died* the *death* of the righteous.
    You *sang a song*.
    I *ran* a *race*.
    She *dreamed a dream*.

2. By denoting a *causative signification*, as:
    They *ran* a *train*.
    He *flew* his *kite*.
    He *flashed* the *powder*.

3. By the *addition* of a *preposition*, as:

Intransitive   *Transitive.*
They laughed *aloud*.   They laughed *at him*.

Transitive, passive voice.
He was *laughed at*.

Note.—The verb and the preposition should be parsed together as a compound verb.

Indirect Object.

Rule VI.—Analysis.

A noun or pronoun, used with a preposition, either expressed or understood, to modify the meaning of a verb, should be called, in analysis, an objective phrase element.

The *indirect* object may be a *noun* or *pronoun* used with a preposition to indicate:

1. The *person* or *thing to whom*, or *to which*, or *for whom*, or *for which* an action is exerted.
2. That *out of which* a thing is made.
3. The *person* or *thing of whom*, or *of which something* is said.

Ex.—He gave a book *to me*.
He gives rain *to the thirsty ground*.
It gives strength *to the cord*.
He made a coat *out of the cloth*.
I wrote a letter *for Mary*.
Mary works *for the society*.
John spoke *of his father*.
John spoke *of his troubles*.
You gave *him* a dollar.

Some verbs may be followed by an *indirect object* only, as:

Speak, work, write, and some *others;*

THE SIMPLE SENTENCE. 61

but the *direct* object is often understood, and may be supplied easily.

Ex.—He spoke *to me.*
I work *for him.*
He writes *for the Journal.*

NOTE.—The infinitive, though it is a phrase element, is, when used as an object of a verb, always a direct object.

MODEL I.

Mr. Long bought some toys for his children.

It is a *proposition;* it is the *combination* of a subject and a predicate.

It is the *expression of a thought* in words, therefore it is a *sentence.*

It is a *simple sentence;* it contains but *one* proposition.

It is a *declarative sentence;* it makes an *affirmation.*

Mr. Long   is the *simple subject;* it is not modified.

Bought   is the *simple predicate;* it is modified by the complex direct objective element, *some toys,* of which *toys* is the *basis,* modified by *some,* a *simple adjective word element.*

    Bought is also modified by *for his children,* an *objective phrase element* (indirect object); *for children* is the *basis; children* is modified by *his,* a simple adjective *word* element.

The *indirect* object is often used to complete the meaning of an *adjective*, as:

> I am anxious *to go.*
> She was desirous *of fame.*
> It is not pleasant *to him.*

When the infinitive is used to complete the meaning of an adjective, it is an *indirect object.*

The preposition should be omitted when the indirect object is placed before the direct.

Ex.—Mr. Long bought his *children* some *toys.*

Sometimes the *indirect* object is used *without* a preposition, when the *direct* object is understood.

Ex.—They paid the *man.*

In the foregoing sentence, the word *man* seems to be a *direct* object; but the real construction will be perceived easily when the *direct* object is supplied.

Ex.—They paid the *money* to the *man.*

MODEL II.

I made a kite out of paper for the boy.

It is a *proposition;* it is the *combination* of a subject and a predicate.

It is the *expression* of a *thought* in *words,* therefore it is a *sentence.*

It is a *simple* sentence; it contains but one proposition.

It is a *declarative* sentence; it makes an **affirmation**.

I is the *simple* subject; it is unmodified.

Made is the *simple* predicate; it is modified by *a kite*, a *complex objective word element* (direct object); *kite* is the *basis;* it is modified by *a*, a *simple adjective word element*.

Made is modified, also, by *out of paper*, a *simple objective phrase element* (indirect object) used to show the material used in the construction of the kite; the basis is *out of paper;* it is not modified. *Out of* is a complex preposition.

Made is modified also by *for the boy*, a *complex objective phrase element* (indirect object) used to show *for whom* the *action* represented by *made* was performed.

NOTE.—Verbs are often followed by several indirect objects, differing, however, in meaning, therefore not *compound*, but each depending *directly* on the verb.

EXERCISES UPON THE INDIRECT OBJECTIVE ELEMENT.

1. Mary gave *her* the flowers.
2. He gathered nuts *for the children*.
3. You are full *of ambition*.
4. He is worthy *of your kindness*.
5. They asked *about going to Europe*.
6. I gave clothes *to the poor*.
7. They paid *her*.
8. I worked *for the public*.
9. You made *a quilt of silk*.
10. They coin money *out of silver*.

Write twenty sentences to illustrate the objective element direct and indirect.

DOUBLE OBJECT.

RULE VII.

When a copulative verb, in the active voice, is followed by a direct object, and some attribute of the direct object, the two combined form a double object, which should be called, in analysis, a double objective element.

The **double object** should be distinguished carefully from:

1. The *compound objective element,* as:
I saw the *comet* and the morning *star.*
I met the *man* and the *boy.*

In these sentences either object may be omitted without affecting the meaning of the other, as:

  I saw the *comet.*
  I met the *boy.*

2. The *direct object* and the *indirect object,* as:

  I plowed the *field for Mr. Jones.*
  I plowed *the field.*
  I plowed *for Mr. Jones.*
  I gave *money to the poor.*
  I gave *money.*
  I gave *to the poor.*

In this construction it is seen, also, that the omission of one of the objects does not change in the least the meaning of the other, but such is not true of the *double object.*

In the *construction* of the *double* object, the *direct* object and the *attributive* object are so closely related that a separation of the one from the other makes, in most cases, an entire change in the meaning of the sentence, as:

They called *him John.*
They called *him.*
They called *John.*
She walks a *queen.*
She walks *fast.*

It will be seen, readily, that the *omission* of the attributive objects in the foregoing sentences makes an entire change in the meaning.

The attributive, or *second* object is not always a noun; it may be:

1. A noun, as: They named her *Mary.*
2. An adjective, as: They made her *happy.*
3. A verb, as: They made her *write.*

The attributive object usually denotes the *result* of some *action* upon the *direct object.*

The *result* of the action, if it be indicated by a noun, denotes *rank, office, capacity, profession, trade,* etc., as:

He anointed David (to be) *king.*
They appointed him *chairman.*
Study made him a *scholar.*
Idleness will make him a *pauper.*

It is sometimes difficult to distinguish the *attributive*

object from the *indirect object*. The following will aid in making the distinction:

1. When the *attributive object* is a *noun*, it denotes *what* the direct object *is*, or *what* it is *supposed to be*, as:

They chose her *queen* of the May.
I thought him a *coward*.

2. When the *attributive object* is an *adjective*, it shows some *quality* or *property* belonging to the *direct object*, which *quality* or *property* is the *result* of some *action* of the subject indicated, by the *verb*, as:

She *baked* the bread *brown*.
It *made* me *happy*.

3. When the *attributive object* is a *verb*, it shows:

(1) Some act *performed*, or *to be performed* by the subject, as:

I heard *him* (to) *repeat* the lesson.
I told the *children to play*.

(2) Some action *received* by the *direct object*, as:

I caused him *to be discharged*.
I heard him *reproved*.
I saw it *taken away*.

Sometimes when the *attribute* is a *noun*, it is the *name* of a new *substance* or *material*, which is the *result* of an entire change of the *substance* or *material* represented by the direct object, as:

They burned the *house* to *ashes*.
Frank broke the *plate* into fifty *pieces*.
She boiled *it* to *jelly*.

The change in substance or material is produced by the action, represented by the verb, upon the direct object.

This *kind* of construction assumes various *forms*, some of them *idiomatic* and very *peculiar*.

Many of them, though household expressions, present great difficulty to those who are not familiar with analysis as:

She pumped the *well dry*.
I talked *myself tired*.
He shot the *bird dead*.
You must *keep* the coffee *hot*.
I worked my *hands weary*.
You must *keep* your hands *clean*.

The double object frequently follows a preposition, and is governed by it, as:

For him to become a good boy seems impossible.

NOTE.—Some authors object to the term, double object, but they fail to supply a better one.

MODEL I.

The Court appointed him guardian.

It is a *simple* sentence; it contains but *one* proposition.
It is a *declarative* sentence; it makes an *affirmation*.

Court is the *simple* subject; it is modified by *the*, a simple *adjective* word element.

Appointed is the *simple* predicate; it is modified by *him guardian*, a *double* objective element; *him* is the *direct* object, and *guardian* is the *attributive object*. *Guardian* is an attribute of *him;* and it is governed by *appointed;* it requires both words (him and guardian) to complete the *predication* of the copulative verb *appointed*.

Note.—In this sentence, and in many sentences containing a copulative verb followed by a double object, the conjunction *as*, or the infinitive *to be*, may be placed *before* the attributive object, but they are used only *to connect* the attributive to the direct object.

The infinitive *to be* is used as a *copula* to join the attributive object to the direct object; it cannot *govern* an object. The participle *being* is sometimes used with *as*.

Ex.—We regarded him *as being* honest.

MODEL II.

Make His paths straight.—Bible.

It is a *simple* sentence; it contains but *one* proposition. It is an *imperative* sentence; it expresses a *command*.

Ye (understood) is the subject; it is unmodified

Make is the *predicate;* it is modified by *His paths straight; paths* is the *direct* object, modified by *His*, a simple adjective word element. *Straight* is the *attributive object* (*to be* is understood); it is an *adjective* attribute of *paths*, called *an object*, because it shows the result of the *action* of the verb make upon *paths*.

MODEL III.

I urged him to study.

It is a *simple* sentence; it contains but *one* proposition.
It is a *declarative* sentence; it makes an *affirmation*.

I   is the subject, unmodified.

Urged   is the *simple predicate;* it is modified by *him to study*, a *double objective element*.
          Him is the *direct* object; the infinitive *to study* is the *attributive object;* it shows the kind of action to be performed by the one denoted by the direct object *him*.

MODEL IV.

He ground it to powder.

It is a *simple* sentence; it contains but *one* proposition.
It is a *declarative* sentence; it makes an *affirmation*.

He   is the *subject;* it is unmodified.

Ground is the *simple* predicate; it is modified by *it to powder*, a double objective element. *It* is the *direct* object, *to powder* is the *attributive* object, which represents the *result* of the action, expressed by the verb *ground*, upon the *direct object*.

The preposition *to* is used to show the relation of *powder* to *it*.

The following sentences may be analyzed according to models given above.

EXAMPLES FOR ANALYSIS.
1. They called *him traitor*.
2. Henry considered *himself* a good *marksman*.
3. His parents named *him Samuel*.
4. I thought *him faithful*.
5. They elected *Pierce president*.
6. You made *him angry*.
7. She swept the *floor clean*.
8. It struck the *man dumb*.
9. He painted the *house white*.
10. She dyed the *cloth blue*.
11. The boy made *him cry*.
12. She kept his *supper warm*.
13. Make the *sleeve large*.
14. She caused *it to be destroyed*.
15. She made *him destroy it*.
16. It turned his *hair gray*.
17. I considered *him a good boy*.
18. He ate the *plate empty*.
19. The sky *grew* a beautiful *red*.
20. Consider the *case settled*.

Write original sentences, to illustrate the double object in the different forms.

THE SIMPLE SENTENCE.

THE ADVERBIAL ELEMENT.

RULE VIII.

A word used to modify the meaning of a verb, a participle, an adjective, or an adverb, by denoting time, place, manner, or degree, should be called, in analysis, an adverbial word element.

The *adverbial element* is not necessary to complete the meaning of the element which it modifies; but it adds strength and elegance to composition, and aids in making the thought clear and definite.

Adverbial word elements (adverbs) are so numerous, and so various in use that almost any desirable shade of meaning may be given to a thought, or an expression.

Ex.—I want to go (the infinitive unmodified).
I want to go *now*.
I want to go *then*.
I want to go *soon*.
I want to go *sometimes*.
I want to go *early*.
I want to go *late*.
I want to go *often*.
I want to go *there*.
I want to go *yonder*.
I want to go *somewhere*.
I want to go *abroad*.
I want to go *hence*.
I want to go *fast*.
I want to go *slowly*.
I want to go *fearlessly*.
I want to go *cheerfully*.
I do *not* want to go.

CLASSES OF ADVERBS.

Adverbs of Time.

Adverbs of *time* answer the questions, *when? how long? how often?* as:

When?	How often?	How long?
now	twice	always
then	thrice	everlastingly
soon	often	forever
late	seldom	forevermore
early	again	eternally
lately	yearly	unceasingly
shortly	quarterly	finally
already	monthly	
hitherto	weekly	
afterward	daily	
recently	hourly	
formerly	annually	
previously	continually	
hereafter	frequently	
ever	occasionally	
never	incessantly	
nevermore	repeatedly	

Adverbs of Place.

Adverbs of *place* answer the questions, *where? whither? whence?*

EXAMPLES.

Where?	Whither?	Whence?
here	yonder	
hither	homeward	Whence is properly answered by adverbial phrases.
there	eastward	
thither	westward	
anywhere	northward	
everywhere	southward	
somewhere	upward	
nowhere	downward	

Adverbs of place are not numerous; adverbial phrases are generally used to answer inquiries for place.

Adverbs of Cause and of Purpose.

There are in reality no adverbs of *cause* or of *purpose*, but there are a few that inquire *for* a cause or a purpose, as:

Why? wherefore? and some phrases, as: *On what account? For what reason?*

Adverbial phrases or clauses must be used to answer such questions.

Ex.—*Why* did you come to town?
I came *to buy* provisions for the workmen.
I came *because you sent for me.*

Adverbs of Manner.

Adverbs of manner answer the question, *how?*

Ex.—*How* does she ride?
She rides gracefully.

Adverbs of manner are very numerous; and many of them are derived from qualifying adjectives.

The most of these end in *ly*, as:

softly	worthily	elegantly
sweetly	loftily	beautifully
nobly	sinfully	perniciously
wisely	charmingly	adequately
freely	fearfully	sorrowfully
swiftly	joyfully	admirably
slowly	cheerfully	violently
greatly	wofully	uniformly
gently	selfishly	exquisitely
badly	cunningly	

The words *well*, *ill*, *hard*, *fast*, *loud*, and some others are used, both as adjectives and as adverbs. It is not difficult to make the distinction.

When used to modify *nouns*, they are *adjectives*, as:

Ex.—A *well* man.—WEBSTER'S DICTIONARY.
> Is your father *well*, the old man of whom ye spake?—GENESIS xliii, 27.
> It was *well* with us in Egypt.—NUMBERS xi, 18.
> Your friends are *well*.—SHAKESPEARE.
> He followed the fortunes of that family and was *well* (in favor) with Henry the Fourth.—DRYDEN.

> There's some *ill* planet reigns.—SHAKESPEARE.
> That's an *ill* phrase.—SHAKESPEARE.
> *Ill* ways, *ill* markets, *ill* neighbors.—BACON.
> He is very *ill*.
> An *ill* wind.—JOHN TUSSER, an English author.
> A *loud* noise, a *loud* voice.
> A *fast* horse, a *fast* lock.
> A *hard* apple, a *hard* time.

When used to modify *verbs*, they are adverbs, as:

> He writes *well*.
> *Ill* fares the land.—GOLDSMITH.
> They sing *loud*.
> The horse runs *fast*.
> She works *hard*.

Well is used more frequently as an *adverb* than as an *adjective*.

Ill is not used so much as an *adjective* in America as it is in England.—*See* ALFRED AYRES, in "The Verbalist."

NOTE.—Both *well* and *ill* are used as predicate adjectives, perhaps more frequently than as modifiers, though, as it has been seen, they are used in both constructions.

Under the head of adverbs of manner may be classed such words as: *headlong, helter-skelter, pell-mell, asunder, lengthwise,* and some others.

Adverbs of Degree and of Quantity.

Adverbs of *degree* and of *quantity* answer the question, *how much?*

>Ex.—It is *very* cold.
>You knew it well *enough.*

Among the adverbs of *degree* and *quantity* in constant use are the following:

as	almost	somewhat	tolerably
so	little	however	exceedingly
too	vastly	scarcely	excessively
quite	greatly	nearly	eminently
much	hardly	entirely	extremely
more	wholly	equally	sufficiently
most	rather	partially	altogether
less	very	largely	especially
least			absurdly

Adverbs of degree and of quantity are used to limit *adjectives* and other *adverbs.*

Modal Adverbs.

Some adverbs modify an entire *clause,* and, sometimes, even an entire sentence.

These adverbs are called *modal adverbs,* because they modify the *manner* of the assertion.

They give peculiar shades of meaning, affecting the degree of certainty or of uncertainty with which a statement is made.

Beginning with *absolute denial*, they may be arranged as follows:

Nay, no, not, no wise.

Possibly.

Perhaps, may be, likely, perchance, peradventure, mayhap, haply, etc.

Probably.

Yea, yes, verily, truly, surely, indeed, doubtless, certainly, assuredly, forsooth.

Adverbs of negation are not numerous.

The first *remove* from absolute denial is indicated by *possibly*, a word which has no exact synonym in the language.

The words in the series beginning with perhaps seem to occupy a place midway between absolute denial and absolute certainty.

Probably has no exact synonym in the language. It indicates only a slight remove from certainty.

Adverbs denoting absolute certainty are somewhat numerous, and many of them are used with *yes* to make an expression emphatic.

NOTE.—In the use of the words *possibly* and *probably*, great care should be taken to make the proper distinction between them.

Possibly modifies an entire expression by denoting that there is only a *little* evidence of the existence of what is stated.

Probably modifies an entire expression by denoting

that there is a *great deal* of evidence of the existence of what is stated.

In the following sentences, it will be clearly seen that the modal adverb in each does not limit *one* word alone, but that it affects the *entire sentence*.

> Do you think it will rain to-day?
> I do *not* think it will rain to-day.

Not, in the sentence above, does not modify *think;* the speaker does not mean to say, *I do not think*, but, *I do not think it will rain to-day.*

You will *not* go to town to-day, only to buy him a knife.

Yes, I will go to town to-day, only to buy him a knife.

In the last two sentences it is evident that the adverbs *not* and *yes* belong to the entire expression, and not to one word alone.

The negative modal adverb *no*, derived from *na* or *ne-a*, must not be confounded with adjective *no*, a shortened form of *nope*.

The modal adverbs, excepting *not*, are usually separated by a comma, or commas, from the rest of the sentence.

Remarks on other Adverbs.

The words *now*, *well*, and *why* are often used entirely out of their ordinary signification, having no grammatical relation to other words. They are then called *independent adverbs.*

Ex.—*Well*, I am satisfied with what I have.

The independent adverb should be separated by a comma from the rest of the sentence.

The word *ago* is often used as an adverb, as:

>He left *long ago*.

It is, however, an old form of the past participle (agone) of the verb *go*, and is generally used as an adjective, as:

>He left a year *ago*.
>He left a long time *ago*.

In each of the foregoing sentences, *ago* modifies the noun which it follows.

When an adverb is used as the *subsequent* term of a preposition, it has the construction of a noun, as:

>For this *once*.
>From *here* to *there*.

The word *there* is often used to introduce a sentence, when the subject follows the verb; it is then an expletive.

It is used only for the sake of euphony, and is not to be considered or disposed of as an element in analysis.

The word *like* is used incorrectly, by some writers, to introduce an adverbial element denoting *resemblance* in the manner of performing *actions*, as:

>It came *like* a whirlwind.

Like cannot be used to denote resemblance of actions, therefore, *as* should be the connective, as:

>It came *as* a whirlwind (comes).

Like should be used only in reference to *resemblance* of objects.

>John is *like* his father.
>My hat is *like* yours.

Like is generally used as a *predicate* adjective, and a preposition is always understood, followed by a noun in the objective.

In the sentence:

I am *like* him,

it is readily seen that the use of the objective pronoun *him* is correct; it is governed by *to* understood; but in the following:

I write *like him*

the incorrectness will be perceived at once; one cannot say I write *like him writes*—it would be absurd. The following is the correct form:

I write *as he does*, or, *as he writes*.

In the following, however, *like* is an adverb, used to modify the entire *clause* following it:

Like as a father pitieth his children, so the Lord pitieth them that fear him.

Adverbs may modify a phrase or an entire clause.

Ex.—Come *to me* (infinitive unmodified).
Come *near to me*.
Deep into that darkness peering.—POE.
Far from the madding crowd's ignoble sway.
—GRAY.
Mary came *after the bell had rung* (clause unmodified).
Mary came *soon after the bell had rung*.

MODEL FOR ANALYSIS.

Perhaps he will go there more willingly hereafter.

It is a *sentence;* it is the expression of a thought in words.

It is a *simple* sentence; it contains but *one* proposition.

It is a *declarative* sentence; it makes an affirmation.

He   is the *subject;* it represents that about which something is affirmed; it is not modified.

Will go   is the simple predicate; it represents what is said of the subject; it is modified by *there,* a simple adverbial word element denoting *place;* it is modified also by *more willingly,* a complex adverbial word element denoting *manner; willingly* is the basis; it is modified by *more,* a simple adverbial word element of *degree. Will go* is further modified by *hereafter,* an adverbial word element of time.

                The entire sentence is modified by *perhaps,* a simple adverbial word element, a modal adverb.

In the model given above each class of adverbs is represented.

Write ten sentences, each containing two adverbs of different classes.

THE SIMPLE SENTENCE.

ADVERBIAL PHRASE ELEMENT.

RULE IX.

Any phrase joined to a verb, a participle, an adjective, or an adverb, to denote time, place, cause, manner, or degree, should be called, in analysis, an adverbial phrase element.

The *phrase* used as an adverbial modifier gives a great variety of shades to the meaning of an expression.

The phrase element is more definite than the word element. In the sentence,

> You must come *early*,

the word *early* is very indefinite; for, to the farmer it may mean before sunrise; but, to the man who lives in a town or a city, and to people in general, it has a different meaning. In the following, however,

> You must come *at daybreak*,
> You must come *at seven o'clock*,
> You must come *at noon*,

there is no possibility of mistaking the meaning.

Adverbial Phrases denoting Time.

Adverbial phrases denoting *time* are numerous. The different relations of time (antecedent, simultaneous, subsequent, and duration) are indicated by the following prepositions:

at	ere	through
after	for	throughout
before	from	till
between	in	toward
betwixt	on	until
by	over	with
during	since	within

Between and *betwixt*, when used to show a relation of time, refer to two points.

Ex.—I shall leave between daybreak and sunrise.

During should be used only when an entire period of time is referred to.

Ex.—I shall remain during the month (all the month).

The words *yesterday*, *to-day*, and *to-morrow* are, by some classed with the adverbial word elements; but they are not adverbs; they are nouns in the objective case, governed by a preposition, either expressed or understood. With the preposition they form adverbial phrase elements of time.

Ex.—I shall go (on) to-morrow.

Before the names of the days of the week *on* is usually either expressed or understood, and *in*, before the names of the months and the years, as:

She came *on* Monday.
She will leave *in* June.
There were four eclipses *in* 1883.

Other prepositions are used with such nouns, also, to indicate certain relations, as:

Since Monday.
Until June.
During the week.

THE SIMPLE SENTENCE.

In the following the preposition is omitted:

> It will last *a second*.
> It will last *two hours*.
> It will last *all day*.
> It will last *a week*.
> It will last *two months*.
> It will last *ten years*.
> It will last *a lifetime*.
> It will last *a century*.

Either *for* or *during* may be supplied before each noun, in the foregoing sentences.

MODEL FOR ANALYSIS.

They waited two days.

It is a *sentence;* it is the expression of a thought in words.

It is a *simple* sentence; it contains but *one* proposition.

It is a *declarative* sentence; it makes an *affirmation*.

They   is the *subject;* it represents that about which something is affirmed; it is unmodified.

Waited   is the *simple* predicate; it is modified by *two days*, a complex adverbial phrase element denoting *duration* of *time;* the preposition (for or during) is understood; *days* is the basis; it is modified by *two*, a simple adjective word element.

EXERCISES UPON THE ADVERBIAL PHRASE DENOTING TIME.

Go *at once*.
Come *to-morrow*.
We are to leave *at daybreak*.
The ship sailed *last week*.
He remained *a month*.
The boy stayed *two hours*.
I saw it *in* 1883.
She will remain *through the year*.
The snow fell *throughout the night*.

Write sentences illustrating the use of the phrase element of time.

Adverbial Phrases Denoting Place.

Adverbial phrases denoting *place* are very numerous.

They add greatly to variety of expression, and, also give definiteness to a statement which the word element cannot give, as will be seen by comparison:

Where is my knife?
It is *here;* it is *there;* it is *yonder;—word element*.

No explanation is required to show the indefiniteness of the words, *here, there*, and *yonder*, for they are household words, which cause a great amount of annoyance in every-day life.

In the following *phrase* elements, the statements are *definite:*

Where is my hat?
It is *on the table*.
It is *in the basket*.
It is *under the chair*.

Adverbial phrases denoting place are introduced by tne following prepositions, and some others:

at	betwixt	from	throughout
along	before	in—into	up—upon
against	behind	of—out of	under
aboard	beneath	to	underneath
by	down	through	within
between			without

Care should be taken to use the right preposition to indicate a relation of place—say, I went *into* the house, not I went *in* the house.

Some of the relations of place indicated by prepositions are the following:

At denotes nearness in respect to locality—I was *at* home; I was *at* the gate; I was *at* church.

Along denotes continuation in a horizontal direction—I went *along* the road.

Toward and *towards* denote direction in a general way—I looked *toward* the mountain; I went *towards* the house.

To denotes a limit reached—I went *to* the house.

Into denotes entrance—I went *into* the house.

In and *within* denote locality within limits—I was *in* the house; I was *within* twenty miles of the place.

The preposition is sometimes omitted before nouns denoting place—I went (to) home.

MODEL FOR ANALYSIS.

He walked along the shore.

It is a *sentence;* it is the expression of a thought in words.

It is a *simple* sentence; it contains but one proposition.

It is a *declarative* sentence; it makes an affirmation.

He is the subject; it is unmodified.

Walked is the *simple* predicate; it is modified by *along the shore*, a complex adverbial *phrase* element of place, denoting continuation in a horizontal direction; *along shore* is the basis; *shore* is modified by *the*, a simple adjective word element.

EXERCISES UPON ADVERBIAL PHRASES DENOTING PLACE.

He lived *at* home.
He drove *along* the road.
She walked *before* me.
I can see it *from* my window.
John sat *in* the arm chair.
Mary walked *into* the room.
She walked *in* the room.
Henry went *through* the orchard.
He lay *on* the ground.
They are *up* stairs.
The man sat *upon* the bench.
The book is *on* the table.

Write twenty sentences to illustrate the various relations of place indicated by different prepositions.

THE SIMPLE SENTENCE.

ADVERBIAL PHRASES DENOTING CAUSE, SOURCE AND PURPOSE.

Phrases denoting *cause, source,* and *purpose* are *not* numerous.

They answer questions *of what? from what cause or source? on account of what? why? wherefore?*

Ex.—He died *of fever.*
  The boy suffered *from thirst.*
  She did not go *for want of means.*
  They went to Europe *to study in the universities.*

Wherefore is seldom used, excepting in poetry.

MODEL FOR ANALYSIS.

The woman died of grief.

It is a *sentence;* it is the expression of a thought in words.

It is a *simple* sentence; it contains but one proposition.

It is a *declarative* sentence; it makes an affirmation.

Woman is the simple *subject;* it is modified by *the,* a simple adjective word element.

Died is the simple predicate; it is modified by *of grief,* a simple adverbial phrase element denoting *cause.*

EXERCISE UPON PHRASES DENOTING CAUSE, SOURCE AND PURPOSE.

  She wept *for joy.*
  They suffered *from hunger.*
  He went to town *to buy a hat.*
  They traveled *for pleasure.*

He was rewarded *for diligence.*
He was punished *for disobedience.*
She went *to hear the lecture.*
The boy worked *for money.*
The boy worked *to support the family.*
The girl fainted *from fright.*
They died *from exposure.*
I went *to get a book.*

NOTE.—The inseparable phrase, in order, followed by an infinitive, is often used to show the relations of purpose.

Ex.—She went to the country *in order to rest.*

Write sentences to illustrate the use of adverbial phrases of cause, source and purpose.

ADVERBIAL PHRASES DENOTING MANNER.

Adverbial phrases of *manner* are numerous, and they vary materially in use.

Under the head of adverbial phrases denoting manner, are classed commonly, phrases denoting:

How a thing is performed	He managed his business *with prudence.*
Accompaniment	He went *with the Master.*
Agency	It was built *by Solomon.*
Authority	It is said *by astronomers* that there will be four eclipses in the year 1883.
Means	He succeeded *by fraud.* She became independent *by industry.*

Instrument	The tree was killed *by lightning*. The bird was killed *by an arrow*.
Measure of time	John is *ten years* old.
Measure of length or distance..	The rod is *four feet* long. It is *six miles* farther.
Degree	She is cautious *to excess*.

In phrases denoting age or measurement, the preposition is seldom expressed.

In the sentence, John is *ten years* old, the adjective *old* is modified by *ten years*, an adverbial phrase element denoting *measure* of *time;* the preposition *by* is understood,—*by* ten years.

And in the sentence, The rod is *four feet* long, the adjective *long* is modified by *four feet*, an adverbial phrase element, denoting *measure* of length; and in the sentence, It is *four miles* farther, the adjective *farther* is modified by *six miles*, an adverbial phrase element denoting measurement of distance, equivalent to *by six* miles.

In elements of measurement, both of time, length and distance, the idea of *degree* is prominent.

Adverbial phrases denoting *modes* of *travel* or *conveyance* are classed with those of manner, as:

on foot; on horseback; by railroad; by steamer; by express; in a wagon; in a carriage; in a balloon.

Phrases used as modal adverbs give great emphasis:

Ex.—by no means,   by all means,
in no wise,   without doubt,
in no case,   with certainty,
on no condition,   beyond doubt,
in great doubt,   in reality,
       in fact.

All phrases of *asseveration* and *appeal*, and every expression having the nature of an *oath*, are classed under the head of *modal adverbial phrases*, as:

Asseveration, *On my honor; on my word of honor.*
Appeal, *By your love for your country; by the memory of your mother; by all you hold dear.*
Oath, *By Jupiter; by the immortal gods. By Mohammed, Prophet of Allah.*

MODEL FOR ANALYSIS.

On my honor, I have told you everything about it.

It is a *sentence;* it is the expression of a thought in words.

It is a *simple* sentence; it contains but *one* proposition.

It is a *declarative* sentence; it makes an affirmation.

I   is the *subject*, unmodified.

Have told is the simple predicate; it is modified by *everything about it*, a complex objective word element (direct object), *everything* is the basis, modified by the simple adjective phrase element, *about it*.

Have told is modified, also, by *you*, an indirect objective phrase element.

The entire expression is modified by the inseparable phrase, *on my honor*, an adverbial phrase element of *asseveration*.

THE SIMPLE SENTENCE. 91

EXERCISE UPON ADVERBIAL PHRASES OF MANNER.

He conducted the campaign *with great skill*.
The men completed the work *with promptness*.
The children went to church regularly *with their parents*.
A wall *six feet* high was built around it.
The Temple was built *by Solomon*.
A boy killed a bird *with a stone*.
John killed an owl *with an arrow*.
The fact is stated *by a London newspaper*.
He is *four years* older.
It is *three miles* farther.
He succeeded by *industry and perseverance*.

NOTE.—Adverbial phrases denoting manner, showing how anything is done, are, the most of them, equivalent to adverbs of manner, as:

with prudence = *prudently*.
with skill = *skillfully*.

Write sentences to illustrate the adverbial phrase element in its various uses.

EXERCISE UPON SIMPLE SENTENCES.

1. Praise ye the Lord!
2. Procrastination is the thief of time.—YOUNG.
3. It was an eve of Autumn's holiest mood.—POLLOK.
4. Man's inhumanity to man
   Makes countless thousands mourn.—BURNS.
5. He became eminent.
6. It was a rosy boy, a little copy of his faithful sire.

7. Well had he slept, never to waken more!
8. The huge pile sunk down at once into the opening earth.
9. Nay, good my lord, try him.
10. The following night the moon took her station still higher.
11. The Lord is my shepherd.
12.   Nature seemed
        In silent contemplation, to adore
        Its Maker. —POLLOK.
13. Concentration is the secret of strength.
14. The heavens declare the glory of God.
15.   I am going, O Nokomis,
      On a long and distant journey,
      To the portals of the Sunset.—HIAWATHA.
16. All was silent again.—LONGFELLOW.
17. The conscious stone to beauty grew.—EMERSON.
18. I am monarch of all.—COWPER.
19. Come gentle spring!—THOMSON.
20. Go!

RULES OF SYNTAX.

Rule I.—The subject of a finite verb must be in the nominative case.

Rule II.—The noun or pronoun connected to the subject of a finite verb, by the copula, must be in the nominative case.

Rule III.—The adjective connected by the copula to the subject must represent some characteristic property of the subject.

Rule IV.—The verbal attribute connected to the subject by the copula must represent some action or state natural to the subject.

Rule V.—The attribute of a proposition, whether substantive adjective, or verbal, must agree with the subject, when joined to it by a copulative verb.

Rule VI.—A verb must agree with its subject in person and number:

 1. The verb must be plural when the members of a compound subject are taken conjointly.

 2. The verb must be singular, when the members of the compound subject are taken separately, if the members are each in the singular number.

 3. If one of the members is plural, and the other, or others, singular, the verb must agree with the one next to it.

Rule VII.—Adjectives are used to limit nouns only.

Rule VIII.—A noun or pronoun joined to another noun, to denote possession, must be in the possessive case.

Rule IX.—A noun or pronoun used with another noun or pronoun, to identify, or to explain, or by way of emphasis, is put by apposition in the same case as that of the noun which it limits.

Rule X.—Participles are used to modify nouns and pronouns, but they retain the signification of the verb, and may be modified as the verb.

Rule XI.—Pronouns must agree in gender, number and person with their antecedent.

Rule XII.—A noun or a pronoun used to complete the meaning of a transitive verb, or the participles of a transitive verb, must be in the objective case.

Rule XIII.—Adverbs are used to modify verbs, participles, adjectives and other adverbs.

Rule XIV.—Prepositions are used to show the relation of a noun or a pronoun to some other word in the sentence.

Rule XV.—The noun or pronoun governed by the preposition must be in the objective case.

Rule XVI.—Coördinate conjunctions are used to join elements of the same rank.

Rule XVII.—Subordinate conjunctions are used to join elements of different rank.

Rule XVIII.—The infinitive has the signification and modifications of the verb, but is used as a noun or an adjective.

Rule XIX.—Independent elements, including interjections, have no grammatical relation to the sentence which they accompany.

RULES OF ANALYSIS.

Rule I.—Any word, whether it be an adjective, a noun, or a pronoun, when joined to the subject to limit or qualify it, must be called, in analysis, an adjective word element.

Rule II.—A noun or a personal pronoun in apposition with another pronoun, must be in the same case; and, in analysis, it should be called an adjective word element.

Rule III.—A noun or a pronoun used to limit a noun in any construction, by denoting possession, must be called, in analysis, an adjective word element.

Rule IV.—A preposition and its object, or an infinitive may be used to limit the meaning of a noun, and in analysis should be called an adjective phrase element.

Rule V.—A word used to complete the meaning of a transitive verb or its participles, is in the objective case, and, in analysis, should be called an objective word element.

Rule VI.—A noun or a pronoun used with a preposition to complete the meaning of a verb, should be called, in analysis, an objective phrase element (indirect object).

Rule VII.—When a copulative verb in the active voice is followed by a direct object, and some attribute of the direct object, the two combined form a double object, which should be called, in analysis, a double objective element.

Rule VIII.—A word used to modify the meaning of a verb by denoting time, place, manner, degree, should be called, in analysis, an adverbial word element.

Rule IX.—Any phrase joined to a verb, a participle, an adjective, or an adverb, to denote time, place, cause, manner, or degree, should be called, in analysis, an adverbial phrase element.

Rule X.—Whenever a substantive clause is used as the subject of a proposition, it should be called, in analysis, a clause subject, and should be disposed of as a noun.

Rule XI.—Whenever the substantive clause is used as the attribute of a proposition, it should be called, in analysis, a substantive clause attribute, and should be disposed of as a noun.

Rule XII.—When a clause is used to modify a noun or a pronoun, or any substantive expression, it should be called, in analysis, an adjective clause element.

Rule XIII.—When an adverb is used to join a dependent clause to a noun in the principal proposition, it should be called a relative adverb; and the clause so joined should be called, in analysis, an adjective clause element.

Rule XIV.—When a clause is used to limit a noun by denoting apposition, it should be called, in analysis, an adjective clause element.

Rule XV.—When a substantive clause is used to complete the meaning of a verb, it is in the objective case, and, in analysis, should be called an objective clause element.

Rule XVI.—When a clause is used to modify the meaning of a verb, a participle, an adjective or an adverb, by denoting time, place, cause, manner, or degree, it should be called, in analysis, an adverbial clause element.

Rule XVII.—When a sentence contains an abridged proposition, it should be called a simple sentence, unless it contains a subordinate proposition also.

Rule XVIII.—When a sentence is composed of independent propositions connected by *and, or, nor*, it should be called, in analysis, a compound sentence.

Rule XIX.—When a sentence consists of a compound subject and a simple predicate, or of a simple subject and a compound predicate, it should be called, in analysis, a partially compound sentence.

THE CLAUSE ELEMENT.

A Clause is a group of words containing a *subject* and a *predicate* used as a sentence element.

The term *clause* should not be applied to the principal proposition in a sentence, but should be restricted to a *proposition* which does not express an entire thought.

A clause should not be called a sentence, as it is an *element* only; but a sentence is the *complete expression* of a thought in words, either spoken or written.

The *clause element* may enter into the construction of a sentence, as:

1. *Subject.*
2. *Attribute.*
3. *Adjective element.*
4. *Objective element.*
5. *Adverbial element.*

Clauses are divided according to their use in the construction of sentences into three classes:

1. *Substantive Clauses.*
2. *Adjective Clauses.*
3. *Adverbial Clauses.*

In the construction of sentences, the clause is used as the part of speech for which it is named, is used.

The substantive clause is used as a noun:

1. Subject nominative:
   That you are doing your duty is evident.

2. Predicate nominative:
   The report was, *that the ship was lost in a storm.*

3. Apposition:
>The report, that *the ship was lost in a storm*, was false.

4. Object of a verb:
>I think *that the lecture will be entertaining.*

5. Object of a preposition:
>Save *that from yonder ivy-mantled tower*, etc.

The *adjective clause* is used to limit the meaning of a noun, and, in many cases, may be changed to an adjective without changing the meaning.

>Ex.—A boy who is idle will never excel,—an idle boy will never excel.

An *adverbial clause* is used to modify the meaning of verbs, participles, adjectives and adverbs.

>Ex.—Go *when the sun rises.*
>He, *leaving before the sun rose*, did not see the burning of *the* mill.
>You are taller *than your brother.*
>They fought as bravely *as their commanders.*

Substantive Clause Used as Subject.

RULE X.

Whenever a substantive clause is used as the subject of a proposition, it should be called, in analysis, a clause subject, and should be disposed of as a noun.

The *clause subject* should be treated as a single word, until *after* the sentence is analyzed; then it should be resolved into its component parts.

A sentence containing a clause subject is not a complex sentence, unless it contain a subordinate clause used as a modifier, for the subject cannot be subordinate to any part of the sentence.

The clause subject is commonly introduced by *that*, as:

That they are not satisfied is evident.

Any kind of clause, however, may be used substantively, as subject, if it is a quotation, as:

Why are you dissatisfied? was my question.
Where thou goest, I will go, was the reply.

The expletive *it* is often used to introduce sentences having clause subjects, as:

It is evident that they are dissatisfied.

The clause subject should not be separated from the predicate by any mark of punctuation, when introduced by *that*.

MODEL.

That the world is full of beauty cannot be denied.

This is a *simple declarative* sentence.

That the world is full of beauty	is the simple subject; it is unmodified.
Can be denied	is the simple predicate.
Not	is a modal adverb; it modifies the entire assertion.

The clause subject, *That the world is full of beauty*, is introduced by *that*, a word which has no modifying power. It is not a connective, for the subject of a proposition cannot be subordinate to *any* part of a sentence.

World   is the simple subject; it is modified by *the*, a simple adjective word element.

Is full   is the simple predicate. *Is* is the copula, and *full* is the adjective attribute. *Full* is modified by *of beauty*, an objective phrase element.

EXERCISE UPON THE CLAUSE AS SUBJECT.

1. Oh, where shall rest be found? has been the cry of many a weary soul.
2. When one should be silent is not easily decided.
3. That I should have taken your advice is now very clear.
4. Whether he will remain until his brother arrives is doubtful.
5. Where have you been? was his question.
6. That John has acted very indiscreetly is not to be denied.
7. May I leave the room? was his request.
8. That the Scriptures were given by inspiration is very evident to one who is earnestly seeking for truth.
9. That the Creator intended to make his creatures happy is proved by his causing the land and the waters, the air, and even the lightning to serve them.
10. "I have been where you sent me" was my reply.
11. That he should have acted in such a way is very strange.
12. It is decided that the journey will be too long for her.
13. It is hoped that the change will benefit him.
14. It is said that he spent a large fortune.
16. That he has succeeded so well is surprising.

EXERCISES.

Write ten sentences containing clause subject.

SUBSTANTIVE CLAUSE AS ATTRIBUTE.

RULE XI.

Whenever the substantive clause is used as the attribute of a proposition, it should be called, in analysis, a substantive clause attribute.

The *clause attribute* is joined to the subject by the copula, just as a word or a phrase attribute is joined.

Ex.—My opinion is, that he deserves the reward for good conduct.

The word *that* is commonly used to introduce the clause attribute; but it has no conjunctive force; it is used merely to introduce the clause.

Direct *quotations* are frequently used as clause attributes.

Ex.—The question was, *Where did you find it?*

Sentences containing clause attributes are simple sentences, if no clause used as a modifier is found in them.

The clause attribute should be separated from the copula by a comma.

MODEL I.

The song was, Oh where shall rest be found.

It is a simple sentence; it contains but one proposition.

It is a mixed sentence; it consists of a declarative proposition, and an interrogative proposition.

The first part of the sentence, including the predicate verb (copula) is declarative; the predicate nominative is interrogative.

The predicate nominative, or substantive attribute, *Oh, where shall rest be found?* is direct quotation.

Song is the subject; it is that of which the substantive attribute, *Oh, where shall rest be found,* is asserted by the copula, *was.*

It is modified by *the*, a simple adjective word element.

Was, Oh where shall rest be found? is the predicate; *was* is the copula; *Oh where shall rest be found?* is the substantive attribute, used to represent the subject in another form.

The predicate is not modified.

Oh where shall rest be found? the attribute of the proposition, when considered alone, is an interrogative sentence; it is used to ask a question.

Rest is the subject; it is unmodified.

THE CLAUSE ELEMENT.

Shall be found — is the simple predicate; it is that which is asserted of the subject it is modified by; *where*, an adverbial word element denoting place; it is also used to ask the question.

Oh — is an interjection; it has no grammatical relation to any word in the sentence, yet its use, simultaneous with the sentence, shows the emotional nature of the question.

MODEL II.

His complaint was, that the cattle had destroyed his field of corn.

It is a simple declarative sentence.

Complaint — is the simple subject; it is modified by *his*, a simple adjective word element.

Was, that the cattle had destroyed his field of corn — is the simple predicate; it is unmodified. *Was* is the copula; *that the cattle had destroyed his field of corn*, is the substantive attribute.

Cattle — is the simple subject of the substantive clause; it is modified by *the*, a simple adjective word element.

Had destroyed is the simple predicate; it is modified by the complex direct objective word element, *his field of corn,* of which *field* is the basis, limited by *his,* a simple adjective word element, and, also, by *of corn,* a simple adjective phrase element.

That is used simply to introduce the substantive clause.

EXERCISE UPON THE CLAUSE AS ATTRIBUTE.

1. The important question now is, Where shall I go?
2. His threat was, *that he would punish* the boy severely.
3. My desire is, that you remain until next week.
4. His text was, The Lord is my shepherd, I shall not want.
5. John's excuse will be, that the key could not be found.
6. The telegram was, "We have crossed the mountains without difficulty."
7. Our expectation is, that the steamboat will arrive to-night.
8. Her remark was, "I cannot endure the severity of the Northern winters."
9. My hope is, that the voyage will benefit her health.
10. The result will be that he will lose his position.
11. The command was, *Shoulder arms!*
12. The consequence will be that all his friends will desert him.

13. My question was, "Why did you not return sooner?"

14. For the last hundred years, one of the first facts taught to any child of American birth is, that Jefferson wrote the Declaration of Independence.

15. The wonder is, that the skies should continue so resplendent for months.

16. The statement of the philosophers is, that the phenomenon cannot be accounted for.

17. The superstition is, that it is an omen of evil.

Complex Sentences.

Complex sentences consist of at least *two* propositions, *one* of which is an *independent* or *principal* proposition, and one *dependent* or *subordinate*.

Ex.—*I must go, if you cannot.*

In complex sentences, the *dependent proposition* is always a *modifier* of the *principal* proposition, or of some part of it; and should be called a subordinate *clause*.

Ex.—*The nuts which the children are gathering under the tree yonder* are chestnuts.

In this sentence the clause introduced by *which* modifies *nuts*; but in the following, the dependent clause modifies the entire principal proposition.

Ex.—*Praise ye the Lord, for He is good; for His mercy endureth forever.*

Complex sentences may contain *several subordinate clauses;* and these clauses may be of *different* kinds.

Ex.—I told him that he must return at noon because the man who wanted to employ him would be here at that time.

In the sentence given there are *four propositions, one principal* and *three subordinate;* an *objective clause*, introduced by *that;* an *adverbial clause* introduced by *because*, and an *adjective* clause introduced by *who*.

The clause used as subject, and the clause used as attribute, as it has been explained before, are not *modifiers*, therefore they do not make a sentence complex.

COMPLEX SENTENCES.

ADJECTIVE CLAUSES INTRODUCED BY RELATIVE PRONOUNS.

RULE XII.

When a clause is used to modify a noun or a pronoun, or any substantive expression, it should be called, in analysis, an adjective clause element.

Many of the clauses used to modify nouns are introduced by *relative pronouns*, which relate to some noun or pronoun in the principal proposition, called the antecedent.

Relative pronouns are never found in independent propositions; but they are sometimes retained, when the subordinate clause is abridged.

Ex.—I have no friend in whom I can confide (full form).
I have no friend in whom to confide (abridged form).

The *simple* relative pronouns are: *who, which, that, what, as,* and *but.*

In the construction of sentences, *who* is used to refer to *persons only*, except in the case of personification.

Ex.—O Moon, thou *who* art queen of the night.

Which refers to things. It is used, also, to refer to persons taken collectively, and in interrogative sentences.

> Ex.—The committee *which* was appointed.
> *Which* boy took the prize?

That may be used with equal propriety to refer to persons or things.

> Ex.—I saw the man *that* sold the horse.
> I saw the money *that* he paid for the horse.

In the construction of sentences, *that* is to be preferred to *who* or *which*, in the following cases:

1. After *who*, for the sake of euphony.

> Ex.—Who *that* sees the glorious heavens by night, etc.

2. After, very, same, all.

> Ex.—He is the *very* man *that* I wish to see.
> This is the *same* book *that* you borrowed.
> These are *all that* you need.

3. After adjectives in the superlative degree.

> Ex.—These are the *best* peaches *that* I ever saw.

4. When the pronoun *it* is used as subject, to represent a noun or a pronoun of any *person, number*, or *gender*, used as a substantive attribute.

> Ex.—It was John *that* broke the pitcher.
> *It* was my neighbor's chickens *that* spoiled my garden.

5. When both persons and things are referred to.

> Ex.—The *men* and the *horses that* were on the boat were saved.

What refers to things, but it may be used as an interrogative adjective to inquire for persons.

>   Ex.—*What* boys were found in the orchard?

What is always a word of *double construction*, when it is used as a relative pronoun.

As, after *many, much, same,* and *such,* is a *relative pronoun*.

>   Ex.—He gave me as *many as* I wanted.
>   I took as *much as* I could use.
>   It is the *same as* it was before.
>   And the Lord added to the church daily, *such as* should be saved.—BIBLE.
>   *Such as* I have give I thee.—BIBLE.

>   Save that from yonder ivy-mantled tower
>   The moping owl doth to the moon complain
>   Of such *as* wandering near her secret bower,
>   Molest her ancient, solitary reign.

The word *as*, in the third line of the stanza above, is a relative pronoun, used to join the subordinate clause to *such*, its antecedent, and it is also, the subject of the verb *molest*.

When *but* is used as a relative pronoun it gives a negative idea to the clause which it introduces.

>   Ex.—There is no rose but has its thorn=There is no rose which has *not* its thorn.

The word *but*, in the following, is used in two clauses as a relative pronoun.

There is no lily of field or vale
But shows the touch of Art Divine,
No sparrow that flies o'er hill or dale
But sings protection for me and mine.

As and *but* are both restrictive, therefore they should not be separated from the antecedent by a comma.

Relative Pronouns when Restrictive and when Not Restrictive.

The **Relative** Pronoun is said to be *restrictive* when the clause which it introduces cannot be changed to an *independent clause*, without a change in the meaning.

It limits a noun in the same way that an adjective *word element* limits it.

Ex.—Plants *which have been kept in a greenhouse* cannot endure even the slight frosts of Spring.
Greenhouse plants cannot endure even the slight frosts of Spring.

No comma should be placed before the relative pronoun when it introduces a *restrictive clause.*

That and *as* are always restrictive.

Ex.—The house *that* I bought yesterday is a cottage.
I will read such books *as* you select for me.

Many clauses, however, introduced by relative pronouns, have no restrictive force.

Such clauses are sometimes called *continuative*, that is, they are used to *add* something to the sentence; and the relative pronoun, introducing the clause, is equivalent to *and he, and it.*

Ex.—He bought a fine horse, which he gave to his son == He bought a fine horse, *and he* gave it to his son.

When the clause is not restrictive, a comma should be placed before the relative pronoun. When the relative clause is restrictive, the *antecedent* of the pronoun is often modified by some word used as a *correlative* of the pronoun.

The following are correlatives so used:

The, this, that, these, those, same, such.

Ex.—*The* horse *which* he gave to his son is a fine one.

This *book that* lies on the table was given to me by your brother.

The adjective clause should, if possible, be placed near the word it modifies.

Ex.—Friendship *which flows from the heart* cannot be frozen by adversity.
It is the friendship of the heart *that* cannot be frozen by adversity.

The second sentence is ambiguous on account of the position of the relative pronoun.

MODELS FOR ANALYSIS.

MODEL I.

Blessed is he that considereth the poor.

It is a complex declarative sentence.

Blessed is he   is the principal proposition.

That considereth the poor	is the subordinate proposition.
He	is the simple subject of the principal proposition; it is modified by *that considereth the poor*, an adjective clause element.
Is blessed	is the predicate; *is*, is the copula, and *blessed* is the adjective attribute.
That	is the subject of the subordinate proposition; it is a relative pronoun, and is used also as a connective.
Considereth	is the simple predicate; it is limited by *the poor*, a complex objective word element; *poor* is the basis, modified by *the*, a simple adjective word element.

MODEL II.

It was not the loss of my property that troubled me.

It is a complex declarative sentence.

It was not the loss of my property	is the *principal* proposition.
It	is the simple subject; it is modified by *that troubled me*, an adjective clause element.

Was loss is the simple predicate. *Was* is the copula, and *loss* is the substantive attribute. *Loss* is modified by *the*, a simple adjective word element, and by *of my property*, a complex adjective phrase element; *of property* is the basis; *property* is modified by *my*, a simple adjective word element.

That is the subject of the subordinate clause; it is used also as a connective.

Troubles is the simple predicate; it is modified by *me*, a simple objective word element.

MODEL III.

There's not a string attuned to mirth,
But has its chord in melancholy.—Hood.

It is a complex declarative sentence.

There's not a string attuned to mirth, is the principal proposition.

But has its chord in melancholy, is the subordinate proposition.

String is the simple subject of the principal proposition; it is modified by *a*, an adjective word element, and by *attuned to mirth*, a complex adjective word element, participial construction. *Attuned* is the basis; it is modified by *to mirth*, an adverbial phrase element.

String is modified also by the adjective clause element, *But has its chord in melancholy*.

Is is the predicate; it denotes existence only. The assertion is modified by *not*, a negative modal adverb. *There* is an expletive, used to introduce the sentence.

But is the subject of the subordinate preposition; it is unmodified. It is a relative pronoun; it has a negative signification, and is equivalent to *that not*.

Has is the simple predicate; it is modified by *its chord*, a complex objective word element; *chord* is the basis, modified by *its*, a simple adjective word element. *Has* is also modified by *in melancholy*, a simple adverbial word element denoting place.

MODEL IV.

He found them prosperous and happy, which surprised him greatly.

This is a complex declarative sentence, consisting of two propositions, one principal, and one subordinate proposition.

He found them prosperous and happy, is the principal proposition; *which surprised him greatly* is the subordinate proposition.

He is the subject of the principal proposition, unmodified.

Found	is the simple predicate; it is modified by *them prosperous and happy*, a double objective element; *them* is the direct object; *prosperous and happy* is a compound adjective attribute, a predicate objective. The entire proposition is the antecedent of *which*, (his finding them prosperous and happy was what surprised him,) and it is modified by *which surprised him greatly*, a simple adjective clause element.
Which	is the subject of the subordinate clause; it is unmodified.
Surprised	is the simple predicate; it is modified by *him*, a simple objective word element, direct object; and by *greatly*, a simple adverbial word element denoting degree.

Compound Relative Pronouns Used to Connect Adjective Clauses.

The *Compound Relative Pronouns* are *whoever, whosoever, whoso, whatever, whatsoever, whichever, whichsoever.*

These words, when used only as relative pronouns, have a double construction, and represent both the antecedent and the relative.

The *antecedent* part of the word belongs to the principal proposition, and the *relative* part introduces the adjective clause.

Ex.—I will send you whatever you want,=I will send you anything which you want.

Note.—It will be seen that the word *whatever* is used indefinitely, and, also, that it expresses the idea with more force and elegance than the equivalent any thing *which*.

All the Compound Relatives are used to express universality.

Whoever=any one who.
Whatever=anything which.
Whichever=either or any of these or those things which.

Whatever and *whichever* are frequently used as adjectives, but they do not lose their office as connectives.

Ex.—They will appreciate whatever kindness you may show them.

Whoever, *whatever* and *whichever* are frequently used with an adversative signification.

Ex.—Whatever the salary may be, I shall not accept the situation.
Whoever may have told you, it is not true.
Whichever you may give him, he will not be satisfied.

In analysis, these clauses should be called *adverbial adversative clauses*.

By some authors, they are called *concessive clauses*.

MODEL.

Whatever you give will be thankfully received.
This is a *complex declarative* sentence.

The antecedent part of *whatever* (equivalent to the thing or the things	is the simple subject of the principal proposition; it is modified by the adjective clause element, which is introduced by the relative part.
Will be received	is the simple predicate; it is modified by *thankfully*, an adverbial element of manner.
You	is the subject of the subordinate proposition; it is unmodified.
Give	is the predicate; it is modified by the *relative part* of the word *whatever*, an objective word element, which is used also as a connective.

Note.—Some authors maintain that such words as the above should not be separated into two parts; but they fail to give a satisfactory analysis of sentences containing them.

EXERCISES UPON THE ADJECTIVE CLAUSE ELEMENT, INTRODUCED BY A RELATIVE PRONOUN.

1. Blessed is the man that walketh not in the counsel of the ungodly.—Psalm I.

2. Ye whose hearts are fresh and simple,
Who have faith in God and Nature,
* * * * * *
Listen to this simple story.—Hiawatha.

3. I picked up these particulars in the course of a journey, which I made some time afterwards.

4. I pity the man who can travel from Dan to Beersheba, and say *"'Tis all barren."*

5. Yonder snow-white cloud that floats in the ether above me
Seems like a hand that is pointing and beckoning over the ocean.—LONGFELLOW.

6. It was a celebrated traveler that related the strange occurrence.

7. It must have been a terrible hurricane that caused the destruction that we see before us.

8. Whoever left it will call for it.

9. Whichever path you take will lead you to the village.

10. The house, in which I live, is a hundred years old.

11. The long galleries were crowded with such an audience as has rarely excited the fears of an orator.

12. There's nothing bright above, below,
From flowers that bloom to stars that glow,
But in its light my soul can see
Some features of the Deity.

13. Broad and brown was the face that under the Spanish Sombrero,
Gazed on the peaceful scene.—LONGFELLOW.

14. The man who alarmed the children this morning, by appearing so suddenly before them, at the door, was an Indian chief.

15. You may have whatever you want.

16. A delightful impression is made upon the stranger who on a bright June day enters the picturesque and charming city of Stockholm.—Du Chaillu.

17. The lofty banner next is seen dispread,
Which bears St. Peter's keys and mitred crown.
—Tasso.

18. How many a poor one's blessing went
With thee beneath the low green tent
Whose curtain never outward swings!
—Whittier.

Write twenty sentences containing adjective clauses introduced by relative pronouns.

Select sentences from a reader containing adjective clauses introduced by *but* and *as*, used as relative pronouns.

Adjective Clauses Introduced by a Relative Adverb.

RULE XIII.

When an adverb is used to join a dependent clause to a noun in the principal proposition, it should be called a **relative adverb**, *and the clause so joined should be called, in analysis, an* **adjective clause element.**

Clauses introduced by relative adverbs are always *restrictive*, and should not be separated from the principal proposition by any mark of punctuation.

Relative adverbs are equivalent to relative pronouns preceded by a preposition.

Ex.—I visited the house *where* he once lived,=I visited the house *in which* he once lived.

The use of the relative adverb as a connective of adjective clauses adds smoothness and beauty to language.

MODEL FOR ANALYSIS.

Shiloh, the place where Joshua set up the tabernacle, and whence he sent surveyors to make a partition of the land, was situated between Lebonah and Bethel.

It is a complex declarative sentence.

It consists of three propositions, one principal, and two subordinate.

Shiloh, the place was situated between Lebonah and Bethel, is the principal proposition.

Where Joshua set up the tabernacle, and whence he sent surveyors to make a partition of the land are the subordinate propositions.

Shiloh is the simple subject of the principal proposition. It is modified by the complex adjective word element, by apposition, *the place where Joshua set up the tabernacle, and whence he sent surveyors to make a partition of the land; place* is the basis; it is modified by the compound adjective clause element, *where Joshua set up the tabernacle, and whence he sent surveyors to make a partition of the land.*

Where Joshua set up the tabernacle — is the first member of the compound adjective clause element. It is introduced by the relative adverb *where*.

Joshua — is the simple subject; it is unmodified.

Set up — is the simple predicate; it is modified by *the tabernacle*, a complex objective word element; *tabernacle* is the basis; it is modified by *the*, a simple adjective word element.

Whence he sent surveyors to make a partition of the land — is the second member of the compound adjective clause element. It is joined to the first member by the coördinate copulative conjunction, *and*. It is introduced by the relative adverb *whence*.

He — is the simple subject; it is unmodified.

Sent is the simple predicate; it is modified, first, by *surveyors*, a simple objective word element; it is also modified by *to make a partition of the land*, a complex adverbial phrase element, denoting purpose; *to make* is the basis, modified by *a partition of the land*, a complex objective word element; *partition* is the basis; it is modified by the simple adjective word element *a;* and also by the complex adjective clause element, *of the land; of land* is the basis; *land* is modified by *the*, a simple adjective word element.

Was situated is the simple predicate of the principal proposition; it is modified by *between Lebonah and Bethel*, an adverbial element of place.

EXERCISES UPON THE ADJECTIVE CLAUSE INTRODUCED BY A RELATIVE ADVERB.

1. And she's gone to the Lake of the Dismal Swamp,
Where, all night long, by a firefly lamp,
She paddles her white canoe.—MOORE.

2. Blest be that spot where cheerful guests retire
To pause from toil and trim their evening fire.
—GOLDSMITH.

3. Patmos, where the apostle John wrote the Apocalypse, is a small island in the Egean Sea.

4. Show me the place where the wild flowers grow.

5. The hour when I shall depart is very near.

6. The time when the boat will arrive is very uncertain.

7. I seek an asylum where I may end my days in peace.

8. The time comes, at last, when the sun disappears entirely from the sight,
when the heavens appear in a blaze of light and glory,
And the stars and moon pale before the Aurora Borealis.—LAND OF THE MIDNIGHT SUN.

9. I long for a home where sorrow never comes!

10. Is there no spot on earth where the weary soul may rest?

11. The Indian loves the land where the wild fowl builds her nest.

12. I once saw the spot where the battle was fought.

13. The boat did not land at the time when it was due.

14. The men who were traveling westward stopped at a place where a fire was burning, to rest, and to take a little refreshment.

15. A deep silence reigned in the house, where in times past, the halls resounded with the sound of mirth.

16. I looked down from the mountain into a valley where cultivated fields and magnificent gardens met the view at every point.

17. Beautiful is that season of life when we can say, in the language of the Scripture: "Thou hast the dew of thy youth."

18. Sublime was the morning that liberty spoke,
And grand was the moment when Spaniards awoke.

19. There's a land far away mid the stars (we are told)
Where they know not the sorrows of time.

Let the pupil write original sentences, containing adjective clauses, introduced by relative adverbs, used to modify the following words

table	moment	time	house
book	college	instant	field
bed	state	city	forest
hour	asylum	place	day

Ex.—It is on the table where the large vase is.

Select sentences from the reader to illustrate this construction, *i. e.*, the sentence containing an adjective clause introduced by a relative adverb.

CLAUSES USED AS ADJECTIVE ELEMENTS BY APPOSITION.

RULE XIV.

When a clause is used to limit a noun by denoting apposition, it should be called, in analysis, an adjective clause element.

Clauses in apposition are often introduced by *that;* but the direct quotation is used, perhaps, as often.

Ex.—The remark that I had offended him, was heard by several of my friends

Your own words, "I will pay for his education," you seem to have forgotten.

The fault, dear Brutus, is not in our stars,
But in ourselves, that we are underlings.

In the foregoing sentence, the word *fault* is modified by *that we are underlings*, a clause used as an adjective element by apposition.

MODEL FOR ANALYSIS.

There is a deep wisdom in the old maxim that truth is to be found in a central point equally remote from divergent errors.

It is a complex declarative sentence.

There is a deep wisdom in the old maxim is the principal proposition.

That truth is to be found in a central point equally distant from divergent errors is the subordinate proposition.

Wisdom is the simple subject; it is modified by *deep*, a simple adjective word element, the complex idea formed by the union of the noun *wisdom* and the adjective *deep; deep wisdom* is modified by the simple adjective word element, *a*.

Is is the simple predicate; it is used to denote existence. It is modified by *in the old maxim that truth is to be found*, etc., an adverbial phrase element, denoting place; *in maxim* is the basis; *maxim* is modified by *old*, a simple adjective word element; and also by the subordinate clause *That truth is to be found*, etc., an adjective clause element by apposition.

COMPLEX SENTENCES.

Truth is the simple subject; it is unmodified.

Is to be found is the simple predicate; *is*, is the copula; it is used to join the attribute, *to be found*, to the subject *truth;* the infinitive attribute (to be found) is used to denote something possible; it is modified by *in a central point, equally distant from divergent errors*, a complex adverbial phrase element; *in point* is the basis; *point* is modified by *central*, a simple adjective word element; the complex idea, *central point*, is modified by *a*, a simple adjective word element. *Point* is modified also by *equally distant from divergent errors*, a complex adjective word element; (this is equivalent to, *which is equally distant*, etc.); *distant* is the basis; it is modified by *equally*, a simple adverbial word element of degree; *distant* is modified, also, by *from divergent errors*, an adverbial phrase element, *from errors* is the basis; *errors* is modified by *divergent*, a simple adjective word element

That is a subordinate conjunction, used to introduce the clause element.

EXERCISES UPON CLAUSES IN APPOSITION USED AS ADJECTIVE MODIFIERS.

1. We hold these truths to be self-evident:
    (1) That all men are created equal;
    (2) That they are endowed by their Creator with certain inalienable rights;
    (3) That among these are life, liberty, and the pursuit of happiness;
    (4) That to secure these rights governments are instituted among men, deriving their just powers from the consent of the governed;
    (5) That whenever any form of government becomes destructive of these ends it is the right of the people to alter or to abolish it, and to institute a new government, laying its foundations on such principles, and organizing its powers in such form as to them shall seem most likely to effect their safety and happiness.—*Declaration of Independence.*

2. The text, He leadeth me beside the still waters, was well managed by the preacher.

3. The hope that he would soon reach home, strengthened him daily.

4. Who does not love that beautiful song, "Jesus, lover of my soul?"

5. The proclamation, that the day should be a day of *thanksgiving*, and not a day of fasting, was received with joy.

6. The news, that the enemy had been forced to retreat, produced great joy in our camp.

7. A rumor, that the enemy had entered the city, spread consternation in every direction.

8. My fear is this, that the promised aid will not reach me in time.

Write original sentences containing clauses in apposition with the following words:

belief, wish, text, song, rumor, intent, thought, opinion, doctrine, conviction, assumption, fear, desire, assertion, demand.

COMPLEX SENTENCES.

Clause Used as Objective Element.

RULE XV.

*When a substantive clause is used to complete the meaning of a verb, it is in the objective case; and, in analysis, should be called an **objective clause element.***

In the following sentences, it will be seen, readily, that the clause elements bear the same relation to the verbs that the word elements bear to them.

>Ex.—I know *John* (objective word element).
>
>I know *that John will come* (objective clause element).
>
>He saw the *basket* (objective word element).
>
>He saw *how the man made the basket* (objective clause element).

That is commonly used to connect the objective clause to the predicate of the principal proposition; but *any* subordinate connective may be so used.

In the case of direct quotation, there is no connective used.

 Ex.—"*Come to me*," he said.

The connective *that* is frequently omitted in indirect quotations used as objective elements; but in analyzing it should be supplied.

 Ex.—He told me the family had left town.

The *substantive clause* is very often used as the object of a *preposition*.

 Ex.—I should have lost my way in the forest, **but** *that I overtook a barefoot boy, who was familiar with the intricate windings of the half-hidden pathway.*
 I had not thought **of** *how easily it might have been saved.*
 You have not heard **of** *where I am going.*

In the first of the foregoing sentences, the clause introduced by *that* is the object of the preposition *but*.

But that I overtook a barefoot boy, etc., is an adverbial element equivalent to *if I had not*, etc.

When the substantive clause is introduced by an interrogative word, the sentence is said to contain an inquiry.

 Ex.—I want to know *why you hesitate.*
 He told me *where he was going.*
 Mary knew *who had taken it.*

A period should be placed at the end of sentences containing an inquiry.

Note.—The substantive clause will be treated of further under the head of Abridged Propositions.

Substantive Clause Used as Objective Element.
(Continued).

QUOTATIONS.

When one uses the language of another for the purpose of illustration, explanation, criticism, or by way of authority, the word, phrase, clause, or sentence so used is called a quotation.

Quotation is said to be *direct* when the exact words of the speaker or writer are used.

Quotation is said to be *indirect* when the thought or opinion of the writer or speaker is given in the language of the one who has borrowed it.

A quotation may consist of one word, or of whole pages.

Where a quotation is long, if direct, it is called *Direct Discourse;* if the quotation is indirect, it is called *Indirect Discourse.*

Quotation marks should be employed to indicate a direct quotation, and, if the quotation be long, a capital letter should be used also.

When a quotation is put within another quotation, it should be indicated by single marks, and if it ends the sentence, the single mark should be followed by the double mark to show that the quotation is complete.

> Ex.—My father said to me once: "Seneca says, 'Economy is, in itself, a great revenue,'" and I believe it.

Quotation marks are not used in the Bible, but all the quotations begin with capital letters.

1*

Ex.—God said, *Let there be light*, and there was light.

And Jesus answering said unto them, *They that are whole need not a physician, but they that are sick.*

A writer may quote his own words and use quotation marks with the same propriety as when quoting from another. The following, though not a clause, is a good illustration:

"Carlo," said I, calling up my dog, into the light, "good fellow, Carlo!"—IK MARVEL.

The *principal proposition* is usually placed first, when the subordinate clause is either direct or indirect quotation.

Ex.—*John said,* "I am not prepared to recite."
John said that he was not prepared to recite.

It may be placed, however, at the end of a sentence, or in the middle of a sentence.

Ex.—"Tell me where you have been," *she said.*
"Let me remain," *said he,* "until to-morrow."

The principal propositions, in some sentences containing quotations, may be changed to subordinate propositions denoting the authority for a statement, without changing the meaning of the statement.

Ex.—He believed, *as he told me,* that the mines would be very valuable.

NOTE.—This kind of construction will be treated of under the head of adverbial elements.

COMPLEX SENTENCES. 131

MODELS FOR ANALYZING SENTENCES CONTAINING QUOTATIONS DIRECT AND INDIRECT.

MODEL I.

Then Judah came near unto him, and said, O my lord, let thy servant, I pray thee, speak a word in my lord's ears.

This is a complex sentence; it is composed of one principal proposition and two subordinate propositions.

It is a mixed sentence; the principal proposition and one of the subordinate propositions are declarative; the leading subordinate proposition is imperative.

Then Judah came near unto him and said   is the principal proposition, which is, also, partially compound, having a compound predicate, *came* and *said*.

Judah   is the subject; it is unmodified.

Came and said   is the grammatical predicate. *Came*, the first member of the compound predicate, is modified by *near unto him*, an adverbial phrase element denoting place. *Unto him* is the basis, modified by *near*, an adverbial word element.

Both members of the compound predicate are modified by the adverbial element *then*, a word element denoting time.

Said, the second member of the compound predicate, is modified by three distinct objective elements, each of which is independent of the other.

O my lord is the direct object of *said*, but is otherwise independent. *Lord* is the basis; it is nominative independent by address; it is limited by *my*, an adjective word element. *O* is used to indicate emotion.

The letter *O* is properly used with the nominative by address.

Said is modified by, *Let thy servant speak a word in my lord's ears*, an objective clause element. This clause is an imperative sentence, and is subordinate only because it is the object of *said*.

Thou (understood) is the subject; it is unmodified.

Let is the predicate; it is modified by *thy servant speak a word in my lord's ears*, a double objective element.

Servant is the direct object, modified by *my*, an adjective word element; (to) *speak a word in my lord's ears* is the complex attributive object.

The basis of the complex attributive object is the infinitive *to speak*, showing something the direct object is to do; it is modified by *a word*, an objective word element; it is modified, also, by *in my lord's ears*, an adverbial phrase element, denoting place; of which, *in ears* is the basis; *ears* is modified by *my lord's*, a complex possessive, used as an adjective element; *lord's* is the basis, modified by *my*, an adjective word element.

Said is further modified by *I pray thee*, a clause used as a direct objective element. Taken alone, it is a complete sentence, and is dependent only because it completes the meaning of *said*. It has no grammatical relation to the other parts of the sentence, but may be considered an element of appeal, used for emphasis.

I is the subject, unmodified.

Pray is the predicate; it is modified by (to) *thee*, an indirect objective phrase element.

MODEL II.

Emerson says that obstinacy is the heroism of little minds.

It is a *complex declarative* sentence.

Emerson says is the principal proposition.

That obstinacy is the heroism of little minds is the subordinate proposition.

Emerson is the subject of the principal proposition; it is unmodified.

Says	is the simple predicate; it is modified by the subordinate clause, *that obstinacy is the heroism of little minds*, an objective clause element, which is joined to the principal proposition by the conjunction *that*.
Obstinacy	is the subject of the subordinate clause; it is unmodified.
Is heroism	is the simple predicate.
Is	is the copula; it is used to join the attribute to the subject.
Heroism	is the substantive attribute; it is modified by *the*, a simple adjective word element. It is modified, also, by *of little minds*, a complex adjective phrase element; *of minds* is the basis; *minds* is modified by *little*, a simple adjective word element.

EXERCISES UPON THE CLAUSE USED AS OBJECTIVE ELEMENT.

1. I know that he will help you.

2. "Well," said the Man of Books, "Your story is not ill told in pleasant verse."—WHITTIER.

3. The Traveler said: "If songs have creeds, their choice of them let singers make."—WHITTIER.

4. He said that he met the man in the depths of the forest.

5. She asked whether the fruit had been brought from the orchard.

6. "Ay, now I comprehend thee, Sancho," said Don Quixote.

7. Thomas Jefferson said: "I know that our legislation, under the regal government, had very many vicious points."

8. I knew that he was in danger of falling.

9. "You are convened this day," he said, "by his Majesty's orders."—MILES STANDISH.

10. But the sly Dwarf said:
"No work is wrought
By Trolls of the hills, O man, for naught."

11. He said that he rested an hour by the wayside.

12. "It is not," he said, "a moral question, but one merely of power."

13. I asked him how far he was going.

14. He replied that he did not know.

15. "Do you know how this stone came here, my friend?" inquired the benevolent Mr. Pickwick.

16. "Is the broth ready?" said Robin.
"No," answered Peggy, "it's not time yet."

17. He said that he had never given the matter a thought.

EXERCISE.

Write ten sentences containing objective clause elements.

Adverbial Clauses.

Rule XVI.

When a clause is used to modify the meaning of a verb, a participle, an adjective, or an adverb, by denoting time, place, cause, manner, or degree, it should be called, in analysis, an adverbial clause element.

The *adverbial* clauses are introduced by *subordinate* conjunctions and *conjunctive adverbs*, of which there is a great *variety*.

Adverbial Clauses Denoting Time.

Adverbial clauses denoting *time* are joined to principal clauses by the following words:

After	as long as	until
as	before	when
as soon as	ere	whenever
as often as	since	while
as frequently as	till	whilst

The words *after, before, ere, since, till* and *until* are classed with the prepositions; but whenever they are used to connect a subordinate clause to a principal clause, they should be called *subordinate conjunctions*.

The first *as*, in each of the following connectives, *as soon as, as often as, as long as*, etc., is an adverb of degree, used to limit the adverbs of *time, soon, often, long*.

The second *as* is a subordinate conjunction, used to connect the subordinate clause to the principal.

Ex.—I came *as soon as* he called me.

COMPLEX SENTENCES. 137

In the foregoing sentence, *as soon* belongs to the principal proposition.

NOTE.—Some regard the words forming these connecives as inseparable; but as the separation may be made so easily, it is perhaps better to regard them as separable.

There are *three divisions* of clauses used to denote time, corresponding to the *absolute* divisions of time, as follows:

1. Time *antecedent, i. e.*, past with regard to the time of the action or event.

Ex.—I heard of it *before* I saw you.

2. Time *simultaneous*, or present with regard to the time of the action or event.

Ex.—*I was there when he came.*

3. Time *subsequent*, or future to the time of the action or event.

Ex.—*I saw him after you left.*

MODELS FOR ANALYSIS.

MODEL I.

Damocles was wishing such delights to endure forever, when he looked up, by chance, and beheld above his head, a sword suspended by a hair.

It is a *complex declarative* sentence.

Damocles was wishing such delights to endure forever is the principal proposition.

When he looked up, by chance, and beheld above his head a sword suspended by a hair, is the subordinate proposition.

6*

Damocles is the subject of the principal proposition; it is unmodified.

Was wishing is the simple predicate; it is modified by *such delights to endure forever;* a complex objective word element, a double object, *delights* is the direct object; it is modified by *such*, a simple adjective word element; *beheld* is the second member of the compound predicate; it is modified by *a sword suspended by a hair; sword* is the basis; it is modified by *a*, a simple adjective word element, and by *suspended by a hair* (abridged from *which was suspended by a hair*), a complex adjective word element, participial construction; *suspended* is the basis; it is modified by, *by a hair*, a complex adverbial phrase element denoting manner; *by hair* is the basis; *hair* is modified by *a*, a simple adjective word element.

Beheld is modified also, by *above his head,* a complex adverbial phrase denoting place; *above head* is the basis; head is modified by *his*, a simple adjective word element; *to endure forever* is the complex attributive object (the attribute of *delights*); *to endure* is the basis, modified by *forever*, a simple adverbial word element, denoting time absolute.

The element, *such delights to endure forever*, is an abridged proposition from the objective clause, *that such delights might endure forever*. The principal proposition is modified by the subordinate adverbial clause element denoting time, *When he looked up, by chance, and beheld, above his head, a sword suspended by a hair.*

He is the simple subject, unmodified.

Looked up and beheld is the compound predicate. *Looked up* is the first member of the compound predicate; it is modified by, *by chance*, a simple adverbial word element denoting manner.

MODEL II.

"*And I must lie here, like a bedridden monk*," exclaimed Ivanhoe, "*while the game that gives me freedom or death is played out by the hand of others.*"

It is a *complex exclamatory* sentence, consisting of four propositions:

1. *Ivanhoe exclaimed.*
2. *And I must lie here, like a bedridden monk.*
3. *While the game is played out by the hand of others.*
4. *That gives me freedom or death.*

Ivanhoe — is the simple subject of the principal proposition; it is unmodified.

Exclaimed — is the simple predicate; it is modified by the remainder of the sentence, a complex objective clause element, direct quotation.

And I must lie here like a bedridden monk — is the basis of the complex objective element.

I — is the simple subject; it is unmodified.

Must lie — is the simple predicate; it is modified by *here*, a simple adverbial word element denoting place.

I — is the simple subject; it is modified by *like a bedridden monk*, a complex adjective word element; *like* is modified by *a bedridden monk*, a complex indirect objective element, completing the meaning of the adjective *like;* (*to* is always understood after *like*) *to monk* is the basis; *monk* is modified

COMPLEX SENTENCES. 141

by *bedridden*, a simple adjective word element.

And is used, not to show any grammatical connection, but simply to indicate a connection in thought with some thought uttered before.

Must lie   is the simple predicate; it is modified by *here*, a simple adverbial word element, denoting place. It is modified, also, by the complex adverbial clause element, denoting time, *while the game that gives me freedom or death, is played out by the hand of others*. *While* is a subordinate conjunction used to join the subordinate clause to the principal clause. It is used also, to modify the verb in each clause. It always denotes duration.

Game   is the simple subject of the principal proposition; it is modified by *the*, a simple adjective word element; it is modified, also, by *that gives me freedom or death*, an adjective clause element.

That   is the subject of the adjective clause, unmodified.

Gives	is the simple predicate; it is modified by *me*, an indirect objective phrase element (*to* is understood before *me*), and by *freedom or death*, a compound direct objective word element. The two members of the compound objective element, *freedom* and *death*, are connected by the coördinate alternative conjunction *or*.
Is played out	is the simple predicate of the adverbial clause; it is modified by, *by the hand of others*, a complex adverbial phrase element denoting the instrument by the use of which something is accomplished; *by hand* is the basis; *hand* is modified by *the*, a simple adjective word element, and by *of others*, a simple adjective phrase element.

MODEL III.

Just as she went down, while her bow was yet recumbent in the dark purple horizon, it is said that an angel appeared standing between her horns.

This is a *complex declarative* sentence, consisting of three propositions, one principal, and two subordinate.

Principal proposition:

That an angel appeared standing between her horns is said.

First subordinate proposition:
Just as she went down.

Second subordinate proposition:
While her bow was yet recumbent in the dark purple horizon.

The principal proposition is introduced by the expletive *it*.

That an angel appeared standing between her horns is the simple subject; it is a clause used as a noun. The clause subject is introduced by the word *that*.

Angel is the subject of the clause (used as subject of the principal proposition); it is modified by *an*, a simple adjective word element; it is also modified by *standing between her horns*, a complex adjective word element, participial construction; *standing* is the basis; it is modified by *between her horns*, a complex adverbial phrase element denoting place; *between horns* is the basis; *horns* is modified by *her*, a simple adjective word element.

The participle *standing* does not modify the predicate; it shows, merely, an accompanying action.

Appeared	is the simple predicate; it is modified by the compound adverbial clause element denoting time, *just as she went down and while her bow was yet recumbent in the dark purple horizon.*
She	is the simple subject of the first member of the compound clause element; it is unmodified.
Went down	is the simple predicate; *went down* is a compound verb, inseparable. *As* is the connective, used also to indicate a point of time simultaneous. The entire clause, *As she went down*, is modified by *just*, a simple adverbial word element.
Bow	is the simple subject of the second member of the compound adverbial clause element; it is modified by *her*, a simple adjective word element.
Was recumbent	is the simple predicate; *was* is the copula; *recumbent* is the adjective attribute; *was recumbent* is modified by *yet*, a simple adverbial word element denoting time; it is also

COMPLEX SENTENCES.

                         modified by *in the dark purple horizon*, a complex adverbial phrase element denoting place; *in horizon* is the basis; *horizon* is modified by *purple*, a simple adjective word element; *purple horizon* is modified by *dark*, a simple adjective word element. (*Dark* and *purple* are two distinct words; there is, however, a compound word, *dark-purple*). *While* is a subordinate connective, used to join the clause, which it introduces, to the principal proposition. It is used, also, to modify *was recumbent;* and *appeared*, by denoting time.

Is said   is the simple predicate of the principal proposition; it is unmodified.

MODEL III.

Will he return as soon as the work is completed?

This is a *complex interrogative* sentence.

Will he return as soon is the principal proposition; *as the work is completed* is the subordinate proposition

He   is the simple subject of the principal proposition; it is unmodified.

Will return is the simple predicate; it is modified by *as soon as the work is completed*, a complex adverbial word element denoting time; *soon* is the basis; it is modified by *as*, a simple adverbial word element, and by *as the work is completed*, an adverbial clause element, used with the first *as* to denote comparison of equality of time; *as* is a subordinate conjunction used to join the subordinate clause to the principal clause.

Work is the simple subject of the subordinate proposition; it is unmodified.

Is completed is the principal predicate, unmodified.

MODEL IV.

You came earlier than John.

This is a *complex* sentence. *You came earlier*, is the principal proposition; *than John* (came early) is the subordinate proposition.

You is the subject of the principal proposition; it is unmodified.

Came is the simple predicate; it is modified by, *earlier than John* (*came early*) a complex adverbial word element donating time; *earlier* is the basis, modified by the adverbial clause element, *than John* (came early) used to denote comparison of inequality.

John is the subject; it is unmodified.

Came is the predicate; it is modified by *early*, a simple adverbial word element.

MODEL V.

Whenever he is left alone in the garden, he does nothing but spoil my flower beds, by running over them to chase the butterflies, and to try to catch the humming birds.

This is a *complex declarative* sentence.

He does nothing but spoil my flower beds by running over them to chase etc.

Whenever he is left alone in the garden is the subordinate proposition.

He is the subject of the principal proposition; it is unmodified.

Does is the simple predicate; it is modified by *nothing but spoil my flower-beds, by running over them to chase the butterflies, and to try to catch the humming birds,* a complex objective word element; *nothing* is the basis; it is modified by *but spoil my flower-beds, by running over them to chase the butterflies, and to try to catch the humming birds,* a complex adjective phrase element; *but* (*to*) *spoil* is the basis; *but* is a preposition, used instead of *except;* (*to*) *spoil* is the object of *but;* (*to*) spoil is modified by *my flower beds,* a complex objective word element; *beds* is the basis, modified by *flower,* a simple adjective word element; and also by *my,* a simple adjective word element. (*To*) *spoil* is modified also by, *by running over them to chase the butterflies, and to try to catch the humming birds*, a complex adverbial phrase element, denoting manner; *by running* is the basis; *running* is modified by *over them*, a simple adverbial phrase element.

Running is a participial noun, in the objective case, governed by the preposition *by*.

Running is modified, also, by to chase the butterflies, and to try to catch the humming birds, a compound adverbial phrase element; (infinitive of purpose) *to chase the butterflies* is the first member of the compound adverbial element of purpose; *to chase* is the basis, it is modified by *the butterflies*, a complex objective word element; *butterflies* is modified by *the*, a simple adjective word element. *To try to catch the humming birds* is the second member of the adverbial element of purpose; *to try* is the basis, modified by *to catch the humming birds*, a complex direct objective phrase element; *to catch* is the basis; it is modified by *the humming birds*, a complex objective word element; *humming birds* is the basis, modified by *the*, a simple adjective word element.

The principal proposition, (entire) is modified by *Whenever he is left alone in the garden*, an adverbial clause element denoting time,

He is the subject; it is unmodified.

Is Left is the simple predicate; *is*, is the copula, and *left* is the verbal attribute.

Is left is modified by *alone*, a simple adverbial element of manner; it is modified also, by *in the garden*, a complex adverbial phrase element, denoting place; *in garden*, is the basis; *garden* is modified by *the*, a simple adjective word element.

Whenever is a conjunctive adverb, used to join the subordinate clause to the principal; it is used also to modify the predicates of both propositions, by denoting time indefinite.

EXERCISES ON THE ADVERBIAL CLAUSE ELEMENT USED TO DENOTE TIME.

1. "Before I was a king," said he, "I was a farmer."—CHARLES XV, OF SWEDEN.

2. When the hour of departure came he accompanied me to the foot of the stairs.

3. When the services were over, many of the audience seemed inclined to linger in the nave, or wander away among the mysterious aisles.—HAWTHORNE.

4. While he was speaking, his voice faltered with emotion.

5. As he approached the house, he heard the sounds of merriment.

6. At length the dial instituted a formal inquiry, when hands, wheels, weights, with one voice, protested their innocence.

7. Leave me, till the twilight comes to soothe my aching heart.

8. As you lift your eyes to the vast amphitheatre, you meet, in imagination, the eyes of a hundred thousand Romans, who have assembled to witness the gladiatorial combats.

9. I must labor until midnight.

10. Can we still set our hearts on the creatures of God, when we find, by sad experience, that the Creator only, is permanent?—Bishop Heber.

11. Harley sat down on a large stone by the way-side to take a pebble from his shoe, when he saw, at some distance, a beggar approaching him.

12. And, as he lay and slept under a juniper tree, behold then an angel touched him.

13. While he was speaking, his voice faltered.

14. Come before the moon rises.

15. I shall remain until I hear from home.

16. Write to him as often as you can.

17. You may leave whenever you desire.

18. Were you at the window as the procession passed by?

19. Remember now thy Creator in the days of thy youth, while the evil days come not, nor the years draw nigh, when thou shalt say, I have no pleasure in them.

20. As we crossed the Sierra Nevada, the snowy mountains that look down upon the luxuriant Vega of Grenada, we overtook a solitary rider, who was singing a wild national song, to cheer the loneliness of his journey.—Longfellow's Prose.

21. When the scorner is punished, the simple is made wise.

22. When Don Quixote was leaving Barcelona, he cast his eye toward the spot where he was thrown.

Write twenty sentences illustrating the different kinds of clause elements denoting time.

Select sentences from the Reader to illustrate the lesson.

Adverbial Clauses Denoting Place.

Adverbial clauses denoting *place* are joined to *principal* clauses by the following *connectives:*

> where,
> wherever,
> where'er,
> wheresoever,
> whither,
> whithersoever,
> whence,
> as far as,
> as long as
> farther than
> longer than.

Where is used to indicate locality.

Ex.—*Let it stay where I placed it.*

Wherever, wheresoever and *where'er*, indicate locality, but in a very indefinite manner.

Ex.—*Wherever you go, I will follow.*

Where'er is used in poetry, rarely in prose.
Whither indicates *direction toward* a place.

Ex.—*Whither thou goest, I will go.*

Whence indicates *direction from a place.*

Ex.—*I know not whence they came.*

Clauses introduced by *whither* and *whence* are not numerous.

They are commonly used as interrogative adverbs.

Ex.—*Whence* come those awful sounds?
Whither dost thou fly, O bird of the silvery wing?

As far as is used to express comparison of equality of distance.

Ex.—We went with him *as far as* the end of the lane.

In *negative comparisons*, *so* should always be used instead of *as*, for the first term of comparison.

Ex.—He did not go with me *so* far as the end of the lane.

Farther than expresses inequality of distance.

Ex.—He went with me *farther than* the end of the lane, (is far.)

MODEL I.

Tired Nature's sweet restorer, balmy Sleep!
He, like the world, his ready visit pays
Where fortune smiles.

This is a *complex declarative* sentence. The first line consists of a noun, in the nominative case, by pleonasm, and its modifiers.

He, like the world, his ready visit pays, is the principal proposition; *Where fortune smiles* is the subordinate proposition.

COMPLEX SENTENCES. 153

Restorer is the nominative case independent by pleonasm (the attention is called to the object before any statement is made about it); it is modified by *sweet*, a simple adjective word element; *sweet restorer* is modified by *Tired Nature's*, a complex adjective element; *Nature's* is modified by *Tired*, a simple adjective word element.

Restorer, is modified, also, by *balmy Sleep*, a complex adjective word element, by apposition; *Sleep* is the basis, modi- by *balmy*, a simple adjective word element.

He is the simple subject; it is modified by *like the world*, a complex adjective word element, *like* is the basis, modified by (*to*) *the world*, a complex indirect objective phrase element; (*to*) *world* is the basis; *world* is modified by *the*, a simple adjective word element.

Pays is the simple predicate; it is modified by *his ready visit*, a complex objective word element; *visit* is the basis, modified by *ready; ready visit* is modified by the simple adjective word element, *his*. *Pays*, is modified, also, by *Where fortune smiles*, a simple adverbial clause element, denoting place; *Where* is the connective, a conjunctive adverb, and, also, modifies the verb in each proposition, *i. e. pays* and *smiles*.

MODEL II.

Wherever you may go, you will find sorrow and disappointment.

This is a *complex declarative* sentence.

You will find sorrow and disappointment, is the principal proposition; *wherever you may go*, is the subordinate proposition.

You — is the subject of the principal proposition; it is unmodified.

Will find — is the simple predicate; it is modified by *sorrow and disappointment*, a compound objective word element, unmodified; the two members of the compound objective element are connected by the coördinate copulative conjunction, *and*. The predicate is modified, also, by *Wherever you may go*, an adverbial clause element, denoting place.

You — is the subject of the subordinate clause, unmodified.

May go — is the simple predicate; it is modified by *wherever*, an adverb of place, which has a universal signification. *Wherever* is also the connective.

EXERCISES UPON ADVERBIAL CLAUSES DENOTING PLACE.

1. Put the trees where they are to be planted.
2. Send it where there is the greatest need.
3. Do you ever go where the basket-makers live?

4. Wherever we are, we are not forgotten by a kind Providence.

5. Where the heart is well guarded, temptations cannot enter.

6. Where the whole is one dark blot of shade, there can be no picture.

7. Whither I go, ye cannot come.

8. Where'er I roam, whatever realms to see,
My heart untravell'd fondly turns to thee.
—GOLDSMITH.

9. He buys where he can get the best bargains.

10. Standing where I was, concealed by the little clump of evergreens, I overheard, *in spite of* myself, the conversation of the two robbers.

11. There is society where none intrudes
By the deep sea, and music in its roar.—BYRON.

12. Where truth and right are concerned, we must not hesitate.

13. Where all were false, I found thee true.
—GEO. P. MORRIS.

14. As far as the eye could reach, the landscape was enchanting in its beauty.

15. The boy stood where he was in danger.

16. The stag at eve had drunk his fill,
Where danced the moon on Monan's rill.
—LADY·OF THE LAKE.

17. Where there is no vigilance, there is no safety.

18. Highest of all, where white peaks glanced,
Where glist'ning streamers waved and danced,
The wanderer's eye could barely view
The summer heaven's delicious blue.   —SCOTT.

19. He not being pleased with the West, will return whence he came.

20. The carrier dove, with willing pinions, flies whither she is sent.

21. I have been where the roses bloom all the year round.

Let the pupil write twenty sentences containing adverbial clauses denoting place.

Adverbial Clauses Used to Denote a Cause or a Reason.

The principal proposition is often modified by an adverbial clause denoting a *cause* or a *reason*.

They are called *causal clauses*.

These clauses are introduced by the conjunctions:

as, because, for, inasmuch as, since.

Ex.—He is rich because he has been industrious and economical.

He must be rich for he lives in luxury.

Since he is so rich, I shall not hesitate to ask his aid.

In the *first* sentence given *above*, the adverbial clause is used to give the real cause of his being rich.

In the *second* sentence, the *adverbial* clause is used to show a reason for making the statement found in the first clause, a reason for drawing the inference.

In the *third* sentence, the adverbial clause shows a reason for not hesitating to ask for aid.

COMPLEX SENTENCES. 157

There is also, another clause, called an illative clause, giving a reason, for the existence of what is stated in the principal clause.

He is rich, therefore he lives in luxury.

MODEL I.

I shall return to the city, at the end of the month, because my business will require my close attention, from that time until the arrival of my partner.

This is a *complex declarative* sentence.

I shall return to the city at the end of the month, is the principal proposition.

Because my business will require my close attention, from that time, until the arrival of my partner, is the subordinate proposition.

I is the simple subject; it is unmodified.

Shall return is the simple predicate; it is modified by *to the city*, a complex adverbial phrase element, denoting place; *to city* is the basis; *city* is modified by *the;*—also by *at the end of the month*, a complex adverbial phrase element, denoting time; *at end* is the basis; *end* is modified by *the*, a simple adjective word element; and by *of the month*, a complex adjective phrase element; *of month*, is the basis; *month* is modified by the simple adjective word element *the*.

Shall return is modified, also, by *because my business will require my close attention, from that time until the arrival of my partner*, an adverbial causal clause, denoting the real cause of his returning.

Business is the simple subject of the subordinate proposition; it is modified by *my*, a simple adjective word element.

Will require is the simple predicate; it is modified by *my close attention*, a complex objective word element (direct object); *attention* is the basis, modified by *close*, a simple adjective word element, *close attention* is modified by *my*, a simple adjective word element.

Will require is modified, also, by *from that time until the arrival of my partner*, a complex adverbial phrase element denoting time. The basis of this element is a phrase, *from that time;* it is modified by *until the arrival of my partner*. The first phrase denotes the beginning of the specified time; the second phrase denotes the end of the specified time.

The basis of the first phrase is *from time; time* is modified by the simple adjective word element *that*.

The basis of the second phrase is *until arrival*, *arrival* is modified by *the*, a simple adjective word element, and by *of my partner*, a complex adjective phrase element; *of partner* is the basis, *partner* is modified by the simple adjective word element *my*.

MODEL II.

They are fighting, for I hear the sound of the artillery.

This is a *complex declarative* sentence.

They are fighting is the principal proposition; *for I hear the sound of the artillery*, is the subordinate proposition.

They is the subject of the principal proposition; it is unmodified.

Are fighting is the simple predicate; the entire expression, *They are fighting*, is modified by, *for I hear the sound of the artillery*, an adverbial causal clause, used to denote the reason for knowing the fact (it does not give the cause, or reason of the fact, that they are fighting).

I is the simple subject of the subordinate clause; it is unmodified.

Hear is the simple predicate; it is modified by *the sound of the artillery*, a complex objective word element; *sound* is the basis, modified by *the*, a simple adjective word element, and by *of the artillery*, a complex adjective phrase element; *artillery* is modified by *the*, a simple adjective word element.

EXERCISE UPON CAUSAL CLAUSES USED AS ADVERBIAL ELEMENTS.

1. I will not prolong the journey, for I am weary and wayworn, and would fain be at Heidelberg, with my readers and my hero.—LONGFELLOW'S PROSE.

2. I came because your horse would come!—JOHN GILPIN.

3. He did not reach here in time, because the train was delayed.

4. Since you have deceived me in such a manner, I cannot trust you again.

5. People often travel many a weary mile in search of happiness, because they do not realize the fact, that it is to be found at their own fireside, where they lost it.

6. The little children, going home from school, did not hesitate to run into her little cottage to escape the rain, for they knew they were always welcome.

7. Since you are not fond of reading, it would be the greatest folly to spend your money, in buying books.

8. As the ship will not sail to-day, our friends will accompany us to the concert to-night.

9. There was no frost last night, for the plants are not injured.

10. He must be sick or absent, for he has not been seen in town this week.

11. Those boys must be very studious, for they always recite well.

12. The Christian religion must be the true religion, for it has stood firm in all ages, in spite of the attacks of unbelievers.

13. As the twilight lingers so long, we may continue our walk.

14. I did not go, because you promised to remain until to-morrow.

15. Since you have confessed your fault, I will forgive you.

16. Because the city did not please him, he moved back into the country.

17. You must leave now to take a little rest, for you look weary, and careworn.

18. I know that he did not bring the package, for I have been here all day, watching anxiously for it.

19. I pitied him, because he had lost the confidence of his master.

20. It is not because one man keeps a coach, while his neighbor walks afoot, that the one is rich, and the other poor.—WEALTH OF NATIONS.

21. It is because one is rich, that he keeps a coach.

22. It is because one is poor, that he goes afoot.

Write sentences to illustrate adverbial causal clauses, introduced by;
    because, since, as, for

Select sentences from the Reader to illustrate the use of the causal clause.

ADVERBIAL CLAUSES DENOTING MANNER.

Adverbial clauses denoting *manner* modify the principal clause by indicating *how* anything is done; and under this head are included:

1. *Correspondence.*
   Ex.—He works as he was directed to work.
2. *Consequence.*
   He works so hard that he cannot endure it long.
3. *Comparison of equality.*
   He works as diligently as any of them.
4. *Comparison of inequality.*
   He works more diligently than any of them.
5. *Comparison of proportionate equality.*
   The harder he works, the more he earns.

Sometimes *two* conjunctions are used together in a sentence, but they have no relation to each other. In such cases, a clause is always omitted by *ellipsis.*

Ex.—Be as courteous to one in humble circumstances, as if you were sure that he would be at no distant day, a man of power and influence.

Expanded form.—

Be as courteous to one in humble circumstances as you would be courteous, if you were sure that he would be, at no distant day, a man of power and influence.

As though is often incorrectly used for *as if.*

Clauses introduced by *as* or *than* always limit the *adjective* or the *adverb* to which they are joined.

The word *as* which precedes the adjective or the adverb, is *itself* an adverb of *degree* used to modify the *word* to which it is joined.—See *Adverbial Clause denoting time.*

Comparison of ***positive*** equality is always indicated by ***as—as.***

Ex.—*John is as tall as James* [is tall].

In comparisons of ***negative*** equality, however, **so**, not *as*, must be used for the *first* term of the comparison.

Ex.—John is not *so* tall as James.

Clauses denoting comparison of *inequality* are introduced by *than*.

Ex.—*He can run faster than you.*

The subordinate clause connected by *than* is used to modify the *adjective* or the *adverb* to which it is joined.

There is usually an ellipsis after *than*, and the noun or pronoun which follows it, must be in the nominative case.

Ex.—No man in the senate is more eloquent than he [is eloquent].

Sometimes both subject and predicate verb are omitted after *than*, leaving only the object.

Ex.—I will call Mary sooner than *him.*

Such expressions as the foregoing, are not considered elegant, though by supplying the subject and predicate the construction will be seen at once:

I will call Mary sooner than I *will call him.*

Proportionate equality is indicated by ***the—the.***

Ex.—*The* faster I ran *the* greater grew my fear.

Adverbial clauses should be separated from principal clauses by a comma, except those introduced by *as* and *than;* clauses connected to the principal proposition by these conjunctions should never be separated by any mark from the principal proposition.

MODELS OF SENTENCES CONTAINING THE DIFFERENT KINDS OF ADVERBIAL ELEMENTS DENOTING MANNER.

MODEL I.

He gave me the medicine, just as you directed.

This is a *complex declarative* sentence.

He gave me the medicine is the principal proposition; *just as you directed,* is the subordinate proposition.

He is the simple subject of the principal proposition; it is unmodified.

Gave is the simple predicate; it is modified by *the medicine,* a complex objective word element (direct object), and by (*to*) *me,* an objective phrase element (indirect object); and, also, by *just as you directed,* an adverbial clause element denoting manner.

You is the subject of the subordinate clause; it is unmodified.

Directed is the predicate; it is unmodified. *As* is a subordinate conjunction used to join the subordinate clause to the principal clause. The entire subordinate clause is modified by *just,* a simple adverbial word element.

MODEL II.

He is not so studious as people suppose.

This is a *complex declarative* sentence.

He is not so studious, is the principal proposition; *as people suppose,* is the subordinate proposition.

He	is the subject of the principal proposition, unmodified.
Is studious	is the simple predicate; *is*, is the copula, and *studious* is the adjective attribute. *Studious* is modified by *so*, an adverbial word element of degree; and by *as people suppose* (*that he is studious*), an adverbial clause element denoting comparison.
People	is the simple subject, unmodified.
Suppose	is the simple predicate, it is modified by the objective clause, understood (that he is studious).

MODEL III.

Then the clouds again changed their color, gradually becoming brighter as if new life had been infused into them. —LAND OF THE MIDNIGHT SUN.

This is a *complex declarative* sentence.

Then the clouds again changed their color, gradually becoming brighter, is the principal proposition; *as if new life had been infused into them,* is the subordinate proposition.

Clouds is the simple subject of the principal proposition; it is modified by *the*, a simple adjective word element, and by *gradually becoming brighter as if new life had been infused into them*, a complex adjective word element, participial construction.

Becoming brighter is the basis; *becoming* is the participle of the copulative verb *become*, followed by *brighter*, a predicate adjective absolute with the participle.

Becoming brighter is modified by *gradually*, a simple adverbial word element of manner (the idea of time is conveyed, also, by *gradually*); it is modified, also, by *as if new life had been infused into them*, a complex adverbial clause element denoting manner.

After *as* an entire proposition is omitted by ellipsis;—*as they would become brighter, if new life had been infused into them*.

The elliptical clause introduced by *as*, is modified by *if new life had been infused*

	into them, a simple adverbial clause element denoting condition.
Life	is the simple subject; it is modified by *new*, a simple adjective word element. If is a subordinate conjunction.
Had been infused	is the simple predicate, it is modified by *into them*, a simple adverbial phrase element of place.
Changed	is the simple predicate of the principal proposition; it is modified by *their color*, a complex objective word element, *color* is the basis, modified by *their*, a simple adjective word element; *changed* is modified, also, by *again*, a simple adverbial element of time.

The participle and its modifiers, besides belonging to the subject, show an accompanying condition, somewhat affecting the predicate.

Models of Sentences Containing Clauses Denoting Comparison of Equality, Comparison of Inequality, of Proportionate Equality of Correspondence, of Consequence and Result.

MODEL I.

The pleasure of seeking it, is as great as the pleasure of finding it.

This is a complex declarative sentence.

The pleasure of seeking it is as great, is the principal proposition; *as the pleasure of finding it (is great),* is the subordinate clause.

Pleasure   is the simple subject of the principal proposition; it is modified by *the*, a simple adjective word element; and by *of seeking it*, a complex adjective phrase element; *of seeking* is the basis,—*seeking* is modified by *it*, a simple objective word element.

Is Great   is the simple predicate; *is* is the copula, and *great* is the adjective attribute. The attribute, *great* is modified by *as*, an adverbial word element of degree, and by *as the pleasure of finding it (is great)*, an adverbial clause element, denoting comparison of equality.

Pleasure   is the simple subject of the subordinate proposition, modified by *the*, a simple adjective word element; and by *of finding it*, a complex adjective phrase element; *of finding* is the basis; *finding* is modified by the simple objective word element *it*.

MODEL II.

As letters some hand hath invisibly traced,
When held to the flame will steal out on the sight,
So, many a feeling that long seemed effaced
The warmth of a meeting like this brings to light.

This is a *complex declarative* sentence, containing five propositions, one principal proposition, and four subordinate propositions.

SUBORDINATE PROPOSITIONS.

1. *The warmth of a meeting like this brings to light, So, many a feeling*—principal proposition,
2. *That long seemed effaced,*
3. *As letters will steal out on the sight,*
4. *(Which) some hand hath invisibly traced,*
5. *When held to the flame,* subordinate propositions.

Warmth is the simple subject of the principal proposition; it is modified by *the*, a simple adjective word element, and by *of a meeting like this*, a complex adjective phrase element; *of meeting* is the basis; *meeting*, is modified by *a*, a simple adjective word element, and by *like this*, a complex adjective word element; *like* is the basis; it is modified by (*to*) *this*, a simple objective phrase element.

Brings	is the simple predicate; it is modified by *many a feeling that long seemed effaced*, a complex objective word element; *feeling* is the basis; it is modified by *many a*, a simple adjective word element; and by *that long seemed effaced,* an adjective clause element.
That	is the simple subject of the adjective clause; it is unmodified.
Seemed effaced	is the simple predicate; *seemed* is a copulative verb, used to join the verbal attribute (to be) *effaced*, to the subject; *seemed effaced*, is modified by *long*, an adverbial word element, denoting time.

Brings is also modified by *to light*, an adverbial phrase element.

The entire expression is limited by *As letters some hand hath invisibly traced, When held to the flame, will steal out on the sight*, a complex adverbial element, denoting manner (correspondence).

Letters is the simple subject of the clause denoting manner; it is modified by *that* (understood) *some hand hath invisibly traced*, an adjective clause element.

Hand is the subject of the adjective clause; it is modified by *some*, a simple adjective word element.

Hath traced is the simple predicate; it is modified by *invisibly*, a simple adverbial word element, and by *that*, a simple objective word element. *That* is also the connective of the adjective clause.

Will steal out is the simple predicate of the principal proposition; it is modified by *on the sight*, an adverbial phrase element. *As* is a connective, used only to join the subordinate clause to the principal. The predicate is modified, also, by *When held to the flame*, an adverbial clause element, denoting time.

They (understood) is the simple subject; it is unmodified.

Are (understood) *held* is the simple predicate; it is modified by *When*, an adverbial word element, denoting time; *when* is used, also, to connect the subordinate clause, denoting time, to the subordinate clause denoting manner. *Are held* is, also, modified by *to the flame*, an adverbial phrase element, denoting place; *to flame* is the basis; *flame* is modified by *the*, a simple adjective word element.

MODEL III.

He was so anxious to return to America that he would not wait an hour longer, though his health was improving rapidly.

This is a *complex declarative* sentence.

He was so anxious to return to America is the principal proposition, *That he would not wait an hour longer, though his health was improving rapidly*, is the complex subordinate clause.

He is the subject of the principal proposition, unmodified.

Was anxious is the simple predicate; *was* is the copula, and *anxious* is the adjective attribute, modified by *so*, an adverbial word element of degree; and by *to return to America*, a complex objective phrase element (in direct object); *to return* is the basis, it is modified by *to America*, an adverbial phrase element, denoting place. The attribute, *anxious*, is modified, also, by *that he would not remain an hour longer, though his health was improving rapidly*, a complex adverbial clause element, denoting consequence.

is the subject, unmodified.

Would remain is the simple predicate; it is modified by *an hour longer*, a complex adverbial word element, denoting time; *longer* is the basis, modified by (by) *an hour*, an adverbial phrase element, denoting measurement of time; the clause is modified by *not*, a modal adverb. The entire clause is modified by *though his health was improving rapidly*, an adversative concessive clause. *That* is a subordinate conjunction, used, only as a connective.

Health is the simple subject of the *concessive* clause; it is modified by *his*, a simple adjective word element.

Was improving is the simple predicate; *was* is the copula, and *improving* is the verbal attribute. The predicate is modified by *rapidly*, an adverbial word element, denoting manner.

Though is a subordinate conjunction, used to join the concessive clause to the denoting consequence.

MODEL II.

He gave me such a look that I was convinced of his sincerity.

This is a *complex declarative* sentence.

He gave me such a look, is the principal proposition; *that I was convinced of his sincerity*, is the subordinate proposition.

He is the subject of the principal proposition, unmodified.

Gave is the simple predicate; it is modified by *such a look*, a complex objective word element; *look* is the basis, modified by *such a* an adjective word element, inseparable; and by *me*, an indirect objective element.

The principal proposition is modified by *that I was convinced of his sincerity*, an adverbial clause element denoting consequence or effect.

COMPLEX SENTENCES. 175

I   is the subject, unmodified.

Was convinced   is the simple predicate; it is modified by *of his sincerity*, a complex objective phrase element (indirect object); *of sincerity* is the basis; *sincerity* is modified by *his*, a simple adjective word element.

MODEL V.

The moon is more beautiful than the sun.

This is a *complex declarative* sentence.

The moon is more beautiful, is the principal proposition; *than the sun* (is beautiful) is the subordinate proposition.

Moon   is the simple subject of the principal proposition; it is modified by *the*, a simple adjective word element.

Is beautiful   is the simple predicate, *is*, is the copula, and *beautiful* is the adjective attribute. *Beautiful* is modified by *more*, an adverbial element of degree, used to form the comparative of *beautiful*.

                More beautiful is modified by *than the sun* (*is beautiful*) an adverbial clause denoting comparison of inequality.

Sun   is the simple subject of the subordinate proposition; it is modified by *the*, a simple adjective word element.

Is beautiful   is the predicate; *Is*, is the copula, and *beautiful* is the adjective attribute. The predicate is unmodified.

MODEL IV.

The further I read, the greater my wonder grew.

This is a *complex declarative* sentence.

The greater my wonder grew, is the principal proposition; and *the further I read*, is the subordinate proposition.

Wonder — is the simple subject of the principal proposition; it is modified by *my*, a simple adjective word element.

Grew greater — is the simple predicate; *grew* is a copulative verb, used to connect the adjective attribute to the subject. *To be* is understood after *grew*. The adjective attribute, *greater*, is modified by *the*, a simple adverbial word element.

The principal proposition is modified by *the further I read*, an adverbial clause element, denoting comparison of proportionate equality.

I — is the subject of the subordinate proposition; it is unmodified.

Read — is the simple predicate; it is modified by *the further*, a complex adverbial word element, denoting distance; it seems, also, to convey the idea of *amount*.

Further is the basis; it is modified by *the* a simple adverbial word element.

EXERCISES UPON ADVERBIAL CLAUSES DENOTING MANNER.

1. He ploughed the fields just as his father ploughed them forty years before.
2. Teach me to labor and to wait as you have done.
3. I can do it just as the carpenter did it.
4. O Time and Change!—with hair as gray
   As was my sire's that winter day,
   How strange it seems, with so much gone
   Of life and love, to still live on!—WHITTIER.
5. I have not seen, in all my wanderings, an apple so good as the golden pippin that grew on the tree by the garden gate.
6. In the depths of the forest are found many wildflowers which are as beautiful as the flowers in the imperial gardens.
7. Your friend has not been so fortunate as you have been.
8. The snow is falling as I have not seen it fall since I left New England.
9. You may manage the affairs of the household during my absence, just as you would manage your own.
10. Suddenly, as if arrested, by a feeling of fear or of wonder.
    Still she stood with her colorless lips apart, while a shudder
    Ran through her frame, and forgotten, the flowerets dropped from her fingers,
    And from her eyes and cheeks, the light and the bloom of the morning.   —EVANGELINE.
11. This stream flows much more rapidly than the stream (that) we crossed this morning.

12. Better is a dry morsel and quietness therewith than a house full of sacrifices with strife.—PROVERBS.

13. It is eighteen degrees colder than it was last night.

14. The colder it grows, the better I feel.

15. The faster I ran, the greater grew my fear.

16. The farther I traveled, the rougher the road became.

17. Are they not more to me than all things else?

18. The longer the nights are, the shorter the time seems.

Write sentences to illustrate the use of *as, just as, than, the—the.*

Let the pupil add clauses denoting consequence or effect, to the following:

> I had so little food.
> He is so tall.
> They are so poor.
> It is so warm.
> The night is so beautiful.
> They gave him such a name.
> The night is so stormy.
> She gave me such a.

ADVERBIAL CONDITIONAL CLAUSES.

An *adverbial clause* is often used to limit the *entire principal clause* by denoting *something necessary* to the *existence* of something *else*.

> Ex.—*The solar system could not keep within its admirable limits for a moment if it were not controlled by an Almighty hand.*

In this sentence, *the solar system, keeping within limits,* is dependent upon a certain condition, *i. e.* that of its being *controlled by an Almighty power.*

Such clauses are called *conditional* clauses.

They are introduced by *if, though, unless, except, provided, provided that,* and *lest.*

The *verb* in the conditional clause is in the subjunctive mode, though it may have the *indicative* or the *potential* form.

MODEL I.

If thou wouldst visit fair Melrose aright,
Go visit it by the pale moonlight.

This is a *complex imperative* sentence.

Go visit it by the pale moonlight, is the principal proposition.

If thou wouldst visit fair Melrose aright, is the subordinate proposition.

Thou	understood, is the simple subject of the principal proposition; it is unmodified.
Go	is the simple predicate; it is modified by (*to*) *visit it by the pale moonlight,* an adverbial element of purpose; the basis is the infinitive *visit* (*to* is understood), modified by *it,* a simple objective word element; *visit* is modified, also, by, *by the pale moonlight,* a com-

plex adverbial phrase element, denoting manner, *by moonlight* is the basis; *moonlight* is modified by *pale*, a simple adjective word element; *pale moonlight* is modified by *the*, a simple adjective word element.

The entire principal proposition is modified by *If thou wouldst visit fair Melrose aright*, an adverbial conditional clause.

Thou is the simple subject of the subordinate clause, unmodified.

Wouldst visit is the simple predicate; it is modified by *fair Melrose*, a complex objective word element; *Melrose* is the basis, modified by *fair*, a simple adjective word element. *Visit* is modified, also, by *aright*, a simple adverbial word element. *If* is a subordinate conjunction used to connect the subordinate clause to the principal.

MODEL II.

Had I known that you were thinking about leaving, I should have advised you to remain.

This is a complex declarative sentence.

I should have advised you to remain; is the principal proposition.

Had I known that you were thinking about leaving, is the subordinate proposition.

I	is the simple subject of the principal proposition; it is unmodified.
Should have advised	is the simple predicate; it is modified by *you to remain*, a double object; *you* is the direct object, and *to remain* is the attributive object. The entire principal proposition is modified by *Had I known that you were thinking about leaving*, a complex subordinate adverbial clause denoting condition, it is equivalent to *If I had known*, etc.
I	is the simple subject of the conditional clause; it is unmodified.
Had known	is the simple predicate; it is modified by *that you were thinking about leaving*, an objective clause element.
You	is the subject of the objective clause, unmodified.
Were thinking	is the predicate; *were* is the copula, and *thinking* is the verbal attribute. *Were thinking* is modified by *about leaving*, a simple objective phrase element (indirect object).

MODEL III.

It will be impossible to reach the place, unless you travel on horseback.

This is a *complex declarative* sentence.

It will be impossible to reach the place, is the principal proposition.

Unless you travel on horseback, is the subordinate proposition.

The sentence is introduced by the expletive *it,* which forms no material part of the sentence.

To reach the place   is the simple subject; it is an infinitive absolute with its modifiers. As subject, it has no modifiers.

Will be impossible   is the simple predicate; the whole expression is modified by the subordinate adverbial clause, *unless you travel on horseback,* denoting condition.

The basis of the subject is *to reach;* it is modified by *the place,* a direct objective word element, place is the basis; it is modified by *the,* a simple adjective word element.

You   is the simple subject of the subordinate clause; it is unmodified.

Travel is the simple predicate; it is modified by *on horseback*, a simple adverbial phrase element.

EXERCISES UPON ADVERBIAL CONDITIONAL CLAUSES.

1. I have no time to spare, for I have much to do.

2. If there were a possibility of having even our free-schools kept a little out of town, it would certainly conduce to the health and vigor of, perhaps, the mind as well as the body.—GOLDSMITH.

3. Had I read as much as others, I might have been as ignorant.

4. If you want to be miserable, think about yourself.

5. Were I to leave him now, I should always regret it, for he needs my attention constantly.

6. Weep not that the world changes,

7. Did it keep
A stable, changeless state, 't were cause indeed to weep.

8. Religion would not have enemies, if it were not an enemy to their vices.

9. Had he listened to the advice of his parents, he would not have been in such distress to-day.

10. If I forgot thee O Jerusalem, let my right hand forget her cunning.—PSALM cxxxvii.

11. If I take the wings of the morning, and dwell in the uttermost parts of the sea, even there shall thy hand lead me.—PSALM cxxxix.

12. The church will be built, provided that enough money be raised.

13. Should the river rise, the large steam-boats would soon be running.

14. He will certainly leave, unless you urge him to remain until he grows stronger.

Write sentences to illustrate the use of the conditional clause, using the following connectives:

If, unless, lest, except, provided that.

Write clauses to limit the following propositions:

John will go to New York.
You may ride.
I cannot remain here.
William can go.
Your plants will wither.
Stand still.
He shall not go.

Write principal propositions, and join to them the following:

Were I in your position.
Had he written one day sooner.
If the moon shine to-night.
Unless you pay in advance.
Provided that the ship sail to-morrow.

ADVERBIAL CLAUSES DENOTING MOTIVE OR PURPOSE.

Adverbial clauses denoting *motive* or *purpose* are not numerous.

They are sometimes called *final* clauses, and are introduced by *that, in order that,* and *lest.*

Not is frequently used in such clause, in connection with *that*, but should not be called a *connective*, though it is so regarded by some authors.

> Ex.—I went that I might avoid the severity of the winter.
>> I went that I might not suffer from the severity of the winter.

The clause denoting purpose is equivalent to an infinitive of purpose.

> Ex.—I went to avoid the severity of the winter.

The clause denoting purpose should be separated from the principal clause by a comma only.

Model of a Sentence Containing an Adverbial Clause Denoting Motive.

Honor thy father and thy mother, that thy days may be long upon the land which the Lord thy God giveth thee.

This is a *complex imperative* sentence. *Honor thy father and thy mother*, is the principal proposition; *that thy days may be long upon the land which the Lord thy God giveth thee* is the complex subordinate clause.

Thou   is the simple subject of the principal proposition; it is unmodified.

Honor   is the simple predicate; it is modified by *thy father and thy mother*, a compound objective word element; the two members of which are joined by the coördinate copulative conjunction *and*. The principal proposition is modified by *that thy days may be

SYNTAX AND ANALYSIS.

long upon the land which the Lord thy God giveth thee, a complex adverbial clause element, denoting motive; *that thy days may be long upon the land* is the basis, *land* is modified by *which the Lord thy God giveth thee*, an adjective clause element.

Days   is the simple subject of the first subordinate clause; it is modified by *thy*, a simple adjective word element.

May be   is the simple predicate; *may* is the auxiliary verb; *be* is used to denote existence; it is, also, modified by *upon the land which the Lord thy God giveth thee*, an adverbial phrase element denoting place; *upon land* is the basis; *land* is modified by *the* a simple adjective word element, and by *which the Lord thy God giveth thee*, an adjective clause element. The entire predicate is modified by *long*, an adverbial word element of duration of time, equivalent to *for a long time*.

Lord   is the simple subject of the adjective clause; it is modified by *thy God*, a complex adjective element by apposition.

Giveth   is the simple predicate; it is modified by (to) *thee*, a simple objective phrase element, indirect object, and by *which*, a simple objective word element, direct object.

EXERCISES UPON ADVERBIAL CLAUSES DENOTING PURPOSE OR MOTIVE.

1. The boy, after laboring hard all day would spend half the night in study, that he might prepare himself to enter college.

2. Be careful, lest what you say be carried abroad "*by a bird* of the air."

3. Take it to a chemist, that he may make an analysis of it.

4. Reprove not a scorner, lest he hate thee.

5. He sat by the window, that he might breathe the pure fresh air, and enjoy the beautiful view of the picturesque scenery round about his home.

6. My father gave me a few acres of land, that I might try the experiment of scientific farming.

7. I brought it, that you might, yourself examine it to see if it is what you want.

8. Do not sell your house, lest you regret it.

9. Obey the voice of conscience, lest thy indifference cause thee sorrow.

10. Be ready, that you may be able to secure a good seat.

11. Read the instructions contained in the letter, that you may know how to proceed.

12. The door of the little church in this strange mountain village, was open when I first saw it, and I entered, that I might be benefited by the atmosphere of devotion which always pervades a house of worship.

13. In order that I might reach home in time, I traveled alone, all night through a dense forest.

Concessive Adverbial Clauses.

A *concessive* subordinate clause is used to modify the *principal* clause by denoting something conceded, yielded, or admitted.

Ex.—Though I meet opposition at every step, I will continue to make the investigation.

The connectives of concessive clauses are:

Although, however, notwithstanding, though.

The *correlatives*, used with these connectives for emphasis, are *nevertheless, still, yet*.

These correlatives are always placed in the principal proposition.

Clauses denoting comparison of equality sometimes express concession.

Ex.— *Weary as I am*, I must continue to work.

Concessive clauses are often introduced by the *compound* relatives, *whatever, whichever, whoever*.

Ex.—Whoever may have told you, it is not true.

MODEL I.

Though he slay me, yet will I trust in him.

This is a *complex declarative* sentence.

Yet will I trust in him, is the principal proposition; *though he slay me*, is the subordinate proposition.

I is the subject of the principal proposition, it is unmodified.

Will trust   is the simple predicate; it is modified by *in him*, an adverbial phrase element of place (this element refers to place in a figurative sense).

                The entire proposition is modified by *Though he slay me*, an adverbial clause element denoting concession.

He   is the subject of the subordinate clause; it is not modified.

Slay   is the simple predicate, it is modified by *me*, a simple objective word element.

                Slay is used instead of *slays*, to put it into the subjunctive form of the verb.

                Though is a subordinate conjunction, used, only to connect the subordinate clause to the principal.

MODEL II.

However content he might seem, his heart was filled with a longing for his mountain home.

This is a *complex declarative* sentence.

His heart was filled with a longing for his mountain home is the principal proposition.

However content he might seem is the subordinate.

Heart   is the simple subject of the principal proposition; it is modified by the simple adjective word element *his*.

Was filled   is the predicate; it is modified by *with a longing for his mountain home*, a complex adverbial element denoting manner; *with longing* is the basis, *longing* (participial noun) is modified by *for his mountain home*, a complex adjective phrase element; *for home* is the basis; *home* is modified by *mountain*, a simple adjective word element; *mountain home* is modified by *his*, a simple adjective word element.

 The entire clause is modified by *However content he might seem*, an adverbial clause denoting concession.

He   is the simple subject, unmodified.

Might seem content   is the simple predicate, *seem* is a copulative verb, used to connect the adjective attribute *content* to the subject; *content*, the attribute, is modified by *however*, a simple adverbial word element.

 However is a conjunctive adverb, it is used, also, to join the subordinate clause to the principal.

EXERCISES UPON ADVERBIAL CONCESSIVE CLAUSES

1. However extravagant he may seem, he really lives within his means.

2. I would not do it, though it would relieve me at once of all embarrassment.

3. Happy as I have been here, I am willing to seek a new home in the west.

4. Whatever farce the boastful hero plays
Virtue alone, has majesty in death.—Young.

5. Poor as he seemed to be, while he lived, he left a large fortune to his heirs.

6. Although I gave him permission to go, I shall not cease to regret it, for I now know that it is impossible for good to result from it.

7. I would not bear such insults a day longer, though it were the means of saving me from a life-time of toil.

Sentences Containing Abridged Propositions.

RULE XVII.

When a sentence contains an abridged proposition, it should be called, in analysis, a simple sentence, unless it contains a subordinate proposition, also.

PARTICIPIAL CONSTRUCTIONS.

Abridge means to shorten, to contract.

With regard to syntax, it does not always refer to the use of fewer words in a sentence; though that is frequently the case.

Abridgment affects the subordinate clause only, changing the construction, but making no material change in the meaning.

The *abridged proposition* adds greatly to the beauty and elegance of language.

The connective *that* is particularly troublesome, as it occurs so frequently in conversation.

It is easy to avoid using it, when one understands abridgment.

>Ex.—He wants *that* I should excuse him.
>I want that you should do me a favor.

These sentences are inelegant; the abridged form is much to be preferred, as:

>He wants me to excuse him.
>I want you to do me a favor.

Propositions are abridged in various ways, when the participial construction is used. In the following the full proposition will be given first:

1. As my home is in the country, I have little opportunity to attend the lectures.

   My home being in the country, I have little opportunity to attend the lectures.

In this sentence, the proposition is abridged by dropping the connective *as*, and changing the verb *is* to the participle *being*; the subject *home* is retained.

2. Your brother did not know that you were here.

   Your brother did not know *of your being here*.

In this example, the connective of the objective clause *that* is dropped; the subject *you* is changed to the possessive *your*; and the verb *were* is changed to the participle *being*.

3. I did not think that it was he.

   I did not think of its being he.

This sentence is like the other, except in one respect; in the first sentence the word *he* is a substantive attribute, in the (predicate) nominative case; and, in the abridged form, it is retained, as predicate nominative absolute with the participle *being*.

4. A little boy, who was named Henry, who was running very rapidly across the field, fell, and hurt himself badly.

A little boy, named Henry, running rapidly across the field, fell, and hurt himself badly.

This sentence contains two subordinate propositions; the first is abridged by dropping the connective and subject *who*, and the copula *was*, and retaining the passive participle, *named*, and the predicate nominative *Henry*.

The second proposition is abridged by dropping the subject *who*, which is, also, the connective and the copula *was*, retaining only the participle *running*, and its modifiers.

5. I considered that he was a good boy.
I considered him as being a good boy.

In this construction, the abridgment is from the objective clause, *that he was a good boy*. It is abridged by dropping the connective *that*, changing the subject *he* to the objective *him*, and the copula *was*, to the participle, *being*, preceded by *as*, a conjunction, used to connect the expression *being a good boy*, to the objective *him; boy* is in the predicate objective connected to the direct object (of which it is an attribute) by the participle of the copula *being*.

Many participles are used in absolute constructions, as:

> Taking it all in all
> Speaking the truth
> Confessing the truth
> Properly speaking

> Ex.—Taking it all in all, we ought to be satisfied.
> Speaking the truth, I know he is in fault.
> Confessing the truth, I am the offender.
> Properly speaking, there is no such thing as a *passive verb*.

There is another form of abridgment, spoken of under the *Phrase Element*, which retains only the adverbial phrase of the clause.

> Ex.—The sunflowers in the garden.—The sunflowers which are in the garden.

The abridged proposition, in any of its forms, always has the name and office of the full proposition.

In the following:

The sunflowers which are in the garden, etc., the subordinate clause, *which are in the garden*, is an adjective *clause* element, used to limit *sunflowers;* and in the abridged form, *in the garden* is used as an adjective *phrase* element, limiting *sunflowers*.

MODELS FOR ANALYSIS.

MODEL I.

On my right, a swelling mountain ridge, covered with verdure, and sprinkled with little white hermitages, looked forth towards the rising sun.

It is a *simple* sentence, containing two abridged propositions, *covered with verdure*, and, *sprinkled with little white hermitages*.

COMPLEX SENTENCES.

The first abridged proposition is changed from the subordinate clause *which was covered with verdure*, to the participial construction, by dropping the subject, *which*, and the copula *was;* retaining the participle and its modifiers, only.

The second abridged proposition is changed in the same manner.

Mountain ridge is the simple subject; it is modified by swelling, an adjective word element, and, also, by the compound adjective word element, participial construction,

Covered with verdure and sprinkled with little white hermitages.

Covered is the basis of the first member of the compound adjective element; it is modified by *with verdure*, an adverbial phrase element, denoting manner; it is unmodified.

Sprinkled with little white hermitages is the second member of the compound adjective element; *Sprinkled* is the basis, modified by *with little white hermitages*, an adverbial phrase element, denoting manner; *with hermitages*, is the basis; *hermitages* is modified by *white*, a simple adjective word element; *white hermitages* is modified by *little*, a simple adjective word element.

Looked forth is the simple predicate. (*Looked* and *forth* combined, form a compound verb—inseparable.)

Looked forth is modified by *on my right*, a complex adverbial phrase element denoting place; *on right* is the basis; *right* is modified by *my*, a simple adjective word element; it is also modified by *toward the rising sun*, a complex adverbial phrase element, denoting direction; *toward sun* is the basis; *sun* is modified by the simple adjective element *rising* (a participial adjective); the complex idea *rising sun* is modified by *the*, a simple adjective word element.

MODEL II.

The moon, coming out from under a cloud, threw her silvery beams all over the landscape, which soon appeared like a scene of enchantment in fairy land.

It is a *complex declarative* sentence

The moon coming out from under a cloud threw her silvery beams all over the landscape, is the principal proposition.

Which soon appeared like a scene of enchantment in fairy land, is the subordinate proposition.

Moon is the simple subject of the principal proposition; it is modified by *the*, a simple adjective word element; it is modified, also, by *coming out from under a cloud*, a complex adjective word element, participial construction; it is an abridged proposition, from *who* (moon is personified) *came out from under a cloud*. *Coming out*, is the basis; it is modified by *from under a cloud*, a complex adverbial phrase element, denoting place; *from under cloud*, is the basis; *cloud* is modified by the simple adjective word element *a*. *From under* is a complex proposition.

Threw is the simple predicate, it is modified by *her silvery beams*, a complex objective word element; *beams* is the basis; it is modified by *silvery*, a simple adjective word element; *silvery beams*, is modified by *her*, a simple adjective word element. The predicate, *threw*, is modified, also, by *all over the landscape, which soon appeared like a scene of enchantment in fairy land; over landscape* is the basis; *landscape* is modified by *the*, a simple adjective word element; also by the adjective clause element, *which appeared like*, etc.

Which is the simple subject; it is unmodified.

Appeared like is the simple predicate. *Appeared* is a copulative verb, used to join the adjective attribute *like* to the subject *which;* it is modified by *soon*, an adverbial word element; *like*, the adjective attribute, is modified by the complex indirect objective phrase element (*to*) *a scene of enchantment in fairy land;* (to) *scene* is the basis; it is modified by *of enchantment*, a simple adjective phrase element; *scene* is, also, modified by *in fairy land*, a complex adjective phrase element (equivalent to *which belongs to fairy land*); *in land* is the basis; *land* is modified by *fairy*, a simple adjective word element.

All is an adverbial element, equivalent to *entirely;* it modifies *over the landscape, which soon appeared*, etc.

MODEL III.

Having witnessed the magnificent sunset, from the top of the mountain, we descended, very slowly, watching the clouds, whose brilliant tints were indescribable.

It is a *complex declarative* sentence, containing an **abridged** proposition.

COMPLEX SENTENCES.

Having witnessed the magnificent sunset from the top of the mountain, we descended very slowly, watching the clouds, is the principal proposition; *whose brilliant tints were indescribable,* is the subordinate proposition.

We — is the simple subject of the principal proposition; it is modified by *watching the clouds,* etc., a complex adjective word element; the participle, *watching,* is the basis; it is modified by *the clouds whose brilliant tints were indescribable,* a complex objective word element; *clouds* is the basis, modified by *the,* a simple adjective word element; it is modified, also, by the adjective clause element, *Whose brilliant tints were indescribable.*

Tints — is the simple subject of the subordinate clause; it is modified by *brilliant,* a simple adjective word element; *whose,* a simple adjective word element, modifies *brilliant tints.*

Were indescribable — is the simple predicate, unmodified.

Descended — is the simple predicate of the principal proposition; it is modified by *very slowly,* a complex adverbial word element of manner; *slowly* is the basis, it is modified by *very* a simple adverbial word element, denoting degree. *Descended* is modified, also, by the abridged proposition, *having witnessed the magnificent sunset from the top of the mountain*, which is abridged from the adverbial clause denoting time—*After we had witnessed the magnificent sunset from the top of the mountain*. The basis of the abridged proposition is *Having witnessed*, it is modified by *the magnificent sunset*, a complex objective word element; *sunset* is the basis, modified by *magnificent*, a simple adjective word element; *magnificent sunset* is modified by *the*, a simple adjective word element.

Having witnessed is modified, also, by, *from the top of the mountain*, a complex adverbial phrase element denoting place; *from top*, is the basis; *top* is modified by *the*, a simple adjective word element, and by *of the mountain*, a complex adjective phrase element.

The participle, *Having witnessed*, really refers to, and modifies *we*, understood; *we having witnessed*, etc., but the entire expression modifies the predicate, by denoting time.

The participle *watching*, although it belongs to, and modifies the noun, is used to denote an action, accompanying the action indicated by the predicate verb *descended*.

Let the pupil make sentences containing abridged propositions; using the following participles:

going,	gone,	having gone
doing,	done,	having done
loving,	loved,	having loved
(being) loved,	loved,	having been loved
seeing,	seen,	having seen
feeling,	felt,	having felt

Ex.—*A little boy going to school was bitten by a fierce dog, belonging to a stranger.*

John, loved by his mother, always obeyed her cheerfully.

The past active participle cannot be used to abridge a proposition.

Exercises Upon Sentences Containing Abridged Propositions.

Participial Constructions.

1. Erelong he came to a river, moving in solemn majesty through the forest.

2. I am a pilgrim, benighted on my way.

3. My friend having left, I determined to remain no longer in such solitude.

4. Through my window comes the delightful fragrance of the honeysuckle and the jessamine, reminding me of a sunny clime, where the air is all the time laden with sweetness.

5. Hearing a cry of pain, I hastened to the door, where I found a little child, who had lost its way.

6. The words uttered by him, in jest, proved to be prophetic.

7. Men resting, and waiting for luck to help them, usually wait in vain.

8. I read the other day, some verses written by an eminent painter, which were original and not conventional.

9. Through the long night she sat watching and waiting for his return.

10. Fearing that I might offend him, I was exceedingly careful, in my conduct, and in my conversation.

11. Sharing in the modern contempt for a superficial learning, he has not wasted his time over dead languages, which he could not hope thoroughly to master.

12. Twilight coming on, the two men emerged from their hiding-place.

13. The lone tree standing in the middle of the prairie, has sheltered many a weary traveler.

14. Having reached the end of our journey, we enjoyed a delightful season of rest.

15. Coming down from the mountain, we had a fine view of the magnificent landscape below.

16. The little girl came into the room weeping.

17. She went away laughing.

18. The poor boy, impoverished by the mismanagement of a faithless guardian, is growing up in ignorance.

19. The boy gathering nuts in the woods, is the son of a farmer who lives in the large house on the hill.

20. I want the inkstand on your table.

21. That beautiful tall tree in the yard was planted by my father, thirty years ago.

22. I was delighted to hear of your being in town again.

23. I often thought of him as being my friend.

24. As there were no windows in this dreary abode, the only light which cheered the darkness within came flickering from the fire upon the hearth, and the smoky sunbeams that peeped down the long-necked chimney.

25. I looked out and beheld a procession of villagers advancing along the road, attired in gay dresses, and marching merrily on, in the direction of the church.

26. We saw oranges ripening on the trees.

27. The winds sighing among the trees, warned us of the approach of winter.

28. Vesper looked forth
From out her western hermitage, and smiled;
And up the east unclouded rode the Moon
With all her stars, gazing on earth intense,
As if she saw some wonder walking there.

ABRIDGED PROPOSITIONS.

Infinitive Constructions.

Infinitive forms are frequently used in the abridgment of subordinate propositions, and, particularly, in objective clause elements.

>Ex.—He wishes that he could be free.
>He wishes to be free.

As the subject in the principal proposition, and that in the subordinate are the same in this sentence, the subject is dropped.

But, in the following, it is changed to the objective, and, with the infinitive, forms a double object.

>Ex.—Mary wanted that he should assist her.
>Mary wanted him to assist her.

The pronoun *him* is the direct object and *to assist her*, the attributive object, or predicate objective.

In such a sentence as the following:

>I ordered him to leave.

Most authors call *him* the subject of the infinitive; but, if the *subject* of a proposition *is that about which something is said*, the word *him* cannot be a *subject*, *for* nothing is affirmed of it; and if the predicate is *that which is affirmed of the subject*, *to leave* cannot be the predicate for the infinitive cannot affirm.

The abridged propositions is frequently introduced by the preposition *for*.

Ex.—That he should act in such a way surprises me.
For him to act in such a way surprises me.

In the abridged form above, the preposition *for* is followed by the double object, *him to act*, etc.

Clauses denoting purpose are often abridged by the infinitive construction.

Ex.—He went to New York that he might get employment.
He went to New York to get employment.

In the following: *I told him that the comet was visible*, *him* is the indirect object, *that the comet was visible*, is the direct object.

The infinitive has but two *tenses,* the *present,* and the *present perfect,* and great care is necessary in order to avoid using the wrong one.

The present infinitive should be used when the action indicated by it, is *simultaneous* with the action asserted by the principal verb; as:

I wanted to go with you to Europe, last year.
I want to go with you to Europe this year.
I know I shall want to go with you to Europe next year.

After the following verbs the present infinitive should always be used; they will not take after them the perfect infinitive.

expect	intend	try
hope	command	endeavor
desire	entreat	attempt
wish	want	etc.
	fail	

The *perfect infinitive* should not be used often, and only when the time indicated by the infinitive is past with regard to the time of the action asserted by the principal verb, as:

> He is said to have succeeded well in his profession last year.
> He ought to have succeeded well last year.

The present infinitive may be used, also, with the verbs in the sentences above.

MODEL I.

I thought him to be honest.

This is a *simple declarative* sentence containing an abridged proposition. The expanded form is, *I thought that he was honest.*

In abridging the clause the connective *that* is dropped, the subject *he* is changed to the objective, and the copula *was* is changed to the infinitive *to be,* which is used as copula to connect the adjective attribute to the objective *him.*

I   is the subject, unmodified.

Thought   is the simple predicate; it is modified by the double objective element, *him to be honest; him* is the direct object, and *honest* is the attributive, connected to *him,* by *to be.*

MODEL II.

They went to see the new building.

This is a *simple* sentence, containing an abridged proposition.

ABRIDGED PROPOSITIONS. 207

The expanded form is *They went that they might see the new building.* The subordinate proposition is abridged by dropping the connective *that*, and the subject *they*; and by changing the finite verb *see* to the infinitive of purpose, *to see.*

They is the subject, unmodified.

Went is the simple predicate; it is modified by *to see the new building*, a complex adverbial phrase element, denoting purpose; *to see* is the basis; it is modified by *the new building*, a complex adverbial word element; *building* is the basis; it is modified by *new*, a simple adjective word element; *new building* is modified by *the*, a simple adjective word element.

MODEL III.

I have sold the house, for you to have enough money to defray your expenses in Europe.

This is a *simple* sentence, containing an abridged proposition. The expanded form is *I have sold the house in order that you might have enough money to defray your expenses in Europe.* In abridging the proposition, the connective, *in order that* is dropped, the subject is retained, the predicate verb *might have* is changed to the infinitive *to have*, and the whole follows the preposition *for*.

I is the subject, unmodified.

Have sold is the simple predicate; it is modified by *the house*, a complex objective word element; *house* is the basis, modified by *the*, a simple adjective word element. *Have sold the house* is modified by *for you to have enough money to defray your expenses in Europe*, a complex adverbial phrase element denoting purpose. *For* is used to govern, not *you* alone, but all that follows; *You to have*, etc., is a double objective element; *you* is the direct object, and *to have*, etc., is the attributive object.

To have is modified by *enough money to defray your expenses in Europe*, a complex objective word element; *money* is the basis; it is modified by *enough*, a simple adjective word element, and by *to defray your expenses in Europe*, a complex adjective phrase element; *to defray* is the basis; it is modified by *your expenses*, a complex objective word element; *expenses* is the basis, modified by *your*, a simple adjective word element.

To defray your expenses is modified by *in Europe*, a simple adverbial word element.

EXERCISES UPON ABRIDGED PROPOSITIONS.

1. He begged to have the privilege of remaining a month longer.

2. She taught her children to obey the laws of the land.

3. The man hoped to be able to redeem his property, before the time should expire.

4. I would travel a thousand miles to see it once more.

5. You will be too late for the train, if you stay to hear the lecture to-night.

6. He did not want to remain, for he knew there would be trouble among the members of the society.

7. Let me rest now!

COMPOUND SENTENCES.

RULE XVII.

When a sentence is composed of independent propositions, connected by and, or, nor, it should be called, in analysis, a compound sentence.

A **Compound Sentence** consists of at least two **independent** propositions.

> Ex.—*By the rivers of Babylon, there we sat down; yea, we wept when we remembered Zion.*
> —Psalm cxxxvii.

These propositions have no *modifying* power.

They (the propositions) should *not* be called *clauses;* for a clause is an *integral* part of a sentence, while these may, each, if taken alone, make a full sentence.

The independent propositions of a compound sentence should be called, in analysis, *members*, not clauses.

The members of Compound Sentences are united by *Coördinate Copulative* Conjunctions, either expressed or understood.

These conjunctions do not modify, yet they always suggest the nature of the member of the sentence in which they are found.

1. *Copulative Conjunctions* suggest *harmony*, as: *and*.
2. *Adversative Conjunctions* suggest opposition or contrast, as: *but*.
3. *Alternative Conjunctions* suggest the leaving out of something, as: *or, nor*.
4. *Causal*.— A cause or reason, as: *for, therefore*.

Ex.—1. They sent a box of clothing to the missionaries, *and* it reached them just before they sailed.

2. They sent a box of clothing to the missionaries, *but* they had sailed before it reached the city.

3. They did not send it in time, *or* the missionaries would have received it; for the express had arrived before they left.

4. The missionaries have not the box of clothing on board; *therefore* they must have sailed before the arrival of the express.

Great care should be taken *to avoid* the use of a copulative conjunction, in joining an adversative member of a compound sentence, to the first number. It will be seen readily that the word *and* should not be used in the *second* of the *foregoing* sentences, for the two members do not *harmonize* in thought.

They show *contrast*, therefore *but* is the appropriate conjunction to be used.

Coördination is made *emphatic* by using associate connections and correlatives.

The *associate* connective must be in the member of the sentence in which the principal conjunction is found, but the *correlative* must be in the *other* members.

Ex.—The late frosts injured the crops; *and* the heavy rains, *also*, are doing much damage.

Not only have the crops been injured by the late frosts, *but great damage* has been done by the *constant* and *heavy* rains.

The adverbs, *only, merely, simply* and *even*, are sometimes used with *but*; and in such sentences, the *second* member of the compound sentence is *copulative*, not *adversative*.

The word *but*, when so used, is equivalent to *and the*.

And is the principal *copulative conjunction;* it is used (either expressed or understood) in almost all cases of copulative coördination.

NOTE.—The coördinate conjunctions are often used to introduce a sentence; they do not, however, indicate any grammatical relation, but a relation of thought.

When the word *therefore* is used as an associate of *and*, it shows that the second member is an inference, a consequence, or a conclusion drawn from the first.

In such sentences *and* is often omitted.

Inference,

Ex.—1. A dark cloud is rising, *therefore* we may expect rain.

Conclusion,

2. The engines cannot reach here in time, *therefore* the building must burn to the ground.

Consequence,

3. The large building was not carefully constructed, *therefore* it could not stand the force of the storm.

Moreover is used to *add to*, and to increase the *force* of an *argument;* also, *to give additional proof* or *reason.*

Ex.—I did not *receive your letter* in time; moreover I was *not able to travel.*

And, when used *alone*, denotes simple coördination; when repeated, however, in a series of coördinate propositions, it gives emphasis.

As well as, when used as a copulative conjunction, is inseparable. It makes the coördination stronger than *and* makes it, but when it joins two nouns in the singular, it requires a singular verb.

As well as is commonly used to connect words and phrases, seldom, clauses.

Ex.—Mary *as well as* her sister is attending school in New York.

NOTE.—Emphatic coördination will be fully explained hereafter. The members of a compound sentence are separated by a comma, if the union is very close; otherwise the semicolon or colon is used.

MODELS FOR ANALYZING SENTENCES HAVING COÖRDINATE COPULATIVE CONSTRUCTIONS.

MODEL I.

I labor and I wait.

This is a *compound declarative* sentence, composed of two independent propositions.

I labor is the first member of the compound sentence; and, *I wait* is the second member.

I   is the subject of the first member of the sentence; it is unmodified.

Labor is the predicate, unmodified.

I   is the subject of the second member, unmodified.

COMPOUND SENTENCES. 213

Wait is the predicate, unmodified. *And* is a coördinate copulative conjunction, used to join the two independent propositions, which harmonize with each other.

MODEL II.

The day is done, and the darkness
Falls from the wings of Night.

This is a *compound declarative* sentence.

The day is done is the first member; *and the darkness Falls from the wings of Night* is the second member.

Day — is the simple subject of the first member of the sentence; it is modified by *the*, a simple adjective word element.

Is done — is the predicate; it is unmodified.

Darkness — is the simple subject of the second member; it is modified by *the* a simple adjective word element.

Falls — is the simple predicate; it is modified by *From the wings of Night*, a complex adverbial phrase element of place. *From wings* is the basis; *wings* is modified by *the*, a simple adjective word element, and by *of Night*, a simple adjective phrase element. *And* is a coördinate copulative conjunction, used to join the two members.

MODEL III.

We had not been long in the camp, when a party set out in quest of a bee-tree, and, being curious to witness the sport, I gladly accepted an invitation to accompany them.
—IRVING.

This is a *compound declarative* sentence; the first member of which is complex; and the second member contains an abridged proposition.

We had not been long in the camp, when a party set out in quest of a bee-tree, in the first member of the compound sentence, and *being curious to witness the sport, I gladly accepted an invitation to accompany them,* is the second member.

We	is the subject of the first member, unmodified.
Had been	is *the simple* predicate. *Had* is the auxiliary verb; *been* is the past participle of the verb *be;* it is used to denote existence. *Had been* is modified by *in the camp,* a complex adverbial phrase element of place; *in camp* is the basis; *camp* is modified by *the,* a simple adjective word element. *Had been in the camp* is modified by *long,* a simple adverbial word element of time—duration; *had been long in the camp* is modified by *not,* a modal adverb; and, also, by *when a party set out in quest of a bee-tree,* an adverbial clause element, denoting a point of time simultaneous.

COMPOUND SENTENCES. 215

Party   is the simple subject of the subordinate clause; it is modified by *a*, a simple adjective word element.

Set out   is the simple predicate; it is modified by *in quest of a bee-tree*, a complex adverbial element, denoting purpose; *in quest of bee-tree* is the basis; (*in quest of* is inseparable); *bee-tree* is modified by *a*, a simple adjective word element.

I   is the simple subject of the second member of the compound sentence; it is modified by *being curious to witness the sport*, a complex adjective word element, participial construction (an abridged proposition). *Being* is the participle of the copula; *curious* is the predicate adjective retained after the participle. *Curious* is modified by *to witness the sport*, a complex indirect objective element. This is used to complete the meaning of the adjective alone, it has no grammatical relation to *being*. *To witness* is the basis, modified by the complex objective word element, *the sport*. *Sport* is modified by *the*, a simple adjective word element.

Accepted   is the simple predicate; it is modified by *an invitation to accompany them*, a complex objective word element; *invitation* is the basis, modified by *an*, a simple adjective word element, and by *to accompany them,* a complex adjective infinitive phrase element; *to accompany* is modified by *them,* an objective word element, direct. *Accepted* is modified, also, by *gladly,* a simple adverbial word element of manner. *And* is a coördinate copulative conjunction used to join the two members of the sentence.

MODEL IV.

God said, Let there be light; and there was light.

This is a *compound mixed* sentence, consisting of three propositions, two independent, and one dependent.

The first member of the compound sentence, *God said, Let there be light,* is complex; *God said* is the principal proposition of the first member of the compound sentence, it is declarative; *Let there be light,* is the subordinate proposition; it is imperative, and is, really, the leading and important fact of the sentence; taken alone, it is an independent proposition; as the object of *said,* it is to be regarded as a dependent proposition.

The second member of the compound sentence, *and there was light,* is simple and declarative.

God is the subject of the principal proposition, in the first member of the compound sentence; it is unmodified.

Said is the simple predicate; it is modified by *Let there be light,* a complex objective clause element

Let is the predicate; it is the imperative absolute, that is, the verb is used without reference to any subject whatever. If *thou* or *ye* be supplied, as subject, neither of them would refer to an antecedent.

Let is modified by *light* (*to*) *be*, a double objective element; *light* is the direct object, and (*to*) *be*, used to denote existence, is the attributive object. *There* is an expletive, used for the sake of euphony.

Light is the subject of the second member of the compound sentence; it is unmodified.

Was is the predicate, unmodified; it is used to state the existence of *light;* *there* is an expletive.

And is a coördinate copulative conjunction, used to unite the two members of the compound sentence.

MODEL V.

I heard the trailing garments of the night
Sweep through her marble halls!
I saw her sable skirts all fringed with light
From the celestial walls!—LONGFELLOW.

This is a *compound exclamatory* sentence, composed of two independent propositions.

The first member is, *I heard the trailing garments of the night sweep through her marble halls.*

The second member is, *I saw her sable skirts all fringed with light.*

I	is the subject of the first member; it is unmodified.
Heard	is the simple predicate; it is modified by *the trailing garments of the night sweep through her marble halls*, a complex objective word element, a double object; *garments* is the direct object; *sweep through her marble halls* is the attributive object. *Garments* is the basis, modified by *trailing*, a simple adjective word element, a participial adjective; *trailing garments* is modified by the adjective word element *the*, and by *of the night*, a complex adjective phrase element; *of night* is the basis; *night* is modified by *the*, a simple adjective word element.
	The basis of the attributive object, is *to sweep;* it is modified by *through her marble halls*, a complex adverbial phrase element, denoting place; *through halls* is the basis; *halls* is modified by *marble*, a simple adjective word element; *marble halls* is modified by *her*, a simple adjective word element.
I	is the subject of the second member of the compound sentence; it is unmodified.
Saw	is the simple predicate; it is modified by *her sable skirts all fringed with light, From the celestial walls*, a complex objective word element, a direct object; *skirts* is the basis, modified by *sable*, a simple adjective word element; *sable skirts* is modi-

COMPOUND SENTENCES. 219

fied by *her*, a simple adjective word element. *Skirts* is modified by *all fringed with light From the celestial walls*, a complex adjective word element, participial construction; *fringed* is the basis, modified by *all*, a simple adverbial word element of degree, equivalent to *entirely;* and by *with light From the celestial walls*, a complex adverbial phrase element of manner; *with light* is the basis, *light* is modified by *From the celestial walls*, a complex adjective phrase element; *from walls* is the basis; *walls* is modified by *celestial*, a simple adjective word element; *celestial walls* is modified by *the*, a simple adjective word element.

EXERCISE UPON COMPOUND SENTENCES.

CÖORDINATE COPULATIVE CONSTRUCTIONS.

1. I have often thought upon death; and I find it the least of all evils.

2. Under the fierce winds, the pines bend their heads; and the mountain snow is swept away, forming immense heights, and hiding everything from sight.

3. At this moment the gates opened, and a peasant woman came out.

4. The sun was delightful; and the branches made that gentle May rustling, which seems to come from nests, even more than from the wind.

5. All stood prepared, and through the long, long night,
Expectant pined for morn's returning ray. —TASSO.

6. Life is real; life is earnest!

7. He looketh upon the earth, and it trembleth; He toucheth the hills, and they smoke.

8. The moon is glorious to-night, and the stars have hidden their faces behind her silvery veil.

9. And ere the early bed-time came
    The white drift piled the window frame;
    And, through the glass, the clothes-lines posts
    Looked in like tall and sheeted ghosts.

10.   We had read
    Of rare Aladdin's wondrous cave,
    And to our own, his name we gave.

11. The hunter marked the mountain high,
    The lone lake's western boundary,
    And deemed the stag must turn to bay,
    Where that huge rampart barred the way.

12. Song soothes our pains;
    And age has pains to soothe.

13. For a few moments, the glow of sunset mingles with that of sunrise, and one cannot tell which prevails.—LAND OF THE MIDNIGHT SUN.

14. He staid not for brake, and he stopped not for stone,
    He swam the Eske River, where ford there was none.

15. The Ocean eagle soared
    From his nest by the white wave's foam,
    And the rocking pines of the forest roared:
    This was their welcome home.

16. Ah! distinctly I remember, it was in the black December,
    And each separate dying ember wrought its ghost upon the floor.

17. All cannot be great; and nobody may reasonably expect all the world to be engaged in lauding his merits.

18. They heard, and were abashed, and up they sprung Upon the wing.—MILTON.

19. Creditors have better memories than debtors; and debtors are a superstitious set—great observers of set days and times.

20. Genius has glue on its hands, and will take hold of a marble slab.

ADVERSATIVE COÖRDINATE CLAUSES.

The second member of a compound sentence often contains a thought which is in entire contrast with that in the first member.

These expressions are called adversative.

They are joined to the first member of the sentence by the adversative conjunction *but*.

The word *but* does not modify, though it always suggests something opposed in some way to, the first statement.

The opposition may be, simply, two contrasted statements.

Ex.—*I did not remain long in France; but spent several months in Italy.*

The second member may contain a statement opposed to the inference that would naturally be drawn from the statement made in the first member.

A feeling of deep sorrow was shown for a little time, but it soon passed away.

Adversative coördination is made *emphatic* by means of the associate connectives:

Yet, still, however, nevertheless, notwithstanding, now, then, and some others.

MODEL I.

I went to the country to remain, only a few days; but I found life there so full of delight that I did not return to the city for a month.

This is a *compound sentence*. It is composed of two members.

I went to the country to remain only a few days is the first member.

I   is the subject, it is unmodified.

Went   is the predicate; it is modified by *to the country*, a complex adverbial phrase element; *to country* is the basis; *country* is modified by *the*, an adjective word element.

                     It is also modified by *to remain only a few days*, an infinitive of purpose used as an adverbial element.

                     To remain is the basis; it is modified by *only a few days*, an adverbial phrase element denoting time; of which [*for*] *a few days* is the basis; it is modified by *only*. The basis of the phrase is *for days*; *days* is limited by *a few*.

The second member of the compound sentence is:

But I found life there so full of delight that I did not return to the city for a month.

It is joined to the first member by the coördinate adversative conjunction *but*, which is used to indicate a thought or result entirely opposed to what is found in the first member.

It is complex; it contains a principal and a dependent proposition.

I found life there so full of delight is the principal proposition.

I is the subject; it is unmodified.

Found is the simple predicate. It is modified by the double object, *life so full of delight that I did not return to the city for a month.*

Life is the direct object; [*to be*] *so full of delight*, etc., is the attributive object. *Full* is the basis, it is an adjective used as predicate objectivitive, belonging to *life;* it is modified by *so*, an adverb of degree, and by *of delight*, an indirect objective element.

Full is also modified by the subordinate clause, *that I did not return to the city for a month*, an adverbial clause element denoting consequence. *That* is a subordinate conjunction, used to join the subordinate clause to the word *full* in the principal clause.

I is the subject; it is unmodified.

Did return is the simple predicate; it is modified by *for a month*, an adverbial phrase element, denoting time. The expression is modified by the modal adverb *not*, an adverbial word element denoting negation.

MODEL II.

*Still stands the forest primeval, but under the shade
 of its branches
Dwells another race, with other customs and language.*

This is a *compound sentence,* consisting of two members.

Still stands the forest primeval, is the first member; and, *but under the shade of its branches, Dwells another race,* is the second member.

Forest   is the simple subject of the first member of the compound sentence; it is modified by *the,* a simple adjective word element, and by *primeval,* also, a simple adjective word element.

Stands   is the simple predicate; it is modified by *still,* a simple adverbial word element, denoting time.

Race   is the simple subject of the second member; it is modified by *another,* a simple adjective word element, and by *with other customs and language,* a compound adjective phrase element; *with customs* is the basis of the first member of the compound adjective element; *customs* is modified by *other,* a simple adjective word element; (with) *language* is the second member, *language* is modified by *other,* understood.

Dwells   is the predicate; it is modified by *under the shade of its branches,* a complex adverbial phrase element of place; *under shade* is the basis, *shade* is modified by *of its branches,* a complex adjective phrase element; *branches* is the basis, modified by *its,* a simple adjective word element.

But is a coördinate adversative connective, used to join the second member, which is used to show a contrast, between the condition of the forest (which is the same now as then) and the condition of the village which is different.

Exercises upon Compound Sentences.

Coördinate Adversative Constructions.

1. The moon has not risen yet; but the stars are very bright.

2. I cannot go; but I will send all that is necessary for their comfort.

3. The important invention is said to have been made in the thirteenth century; but it was not in common use until the fourteenth, or even the beginning of the fifteenth century.

4. The truest help we can render to an afflicted man, is not to take his burden from him, but to call out his best strength, that he may be able to bear the burden.

5. Pleasure may fill up the interstices of life, but it is poor material to build its frame-work out of.

6. He went, but did not remain long.

7. We promise according to our hopes; but perform according to our fears.

8. As usual in all congregations, some fell asleep; but in my pew a sleeper was aroused by a pinch of snuff.

9. There was no servility of manner; but all were courteous.

10.   I would make
    Reason my guide, but she should sometimes sit
    Patiently by the wayside, while I traced
    The mazes of the pleasant wilderness
    Around me.   —Bryant.

Alternative Coördinations.

*Coördination is **alternative*** when the members of a compound sentence are considered separately; only one of them containing a statement of a fact; but it is impossible to know from the construction, which contains it.

> Ex.—*I will buy your part of the land, or I will sell you mine.*

Sometimes it is necessary to give a negative signification to alternative coördination.

> Ex.—*I will not sell my part of the land, nor will I buy yours.*

Alternative coördination is made emphatic by using with the principal conjunctions, associate connectives or correlatives; sometimes by both.

> Ex.—*I will either buy your part of the land, or else sell you mine.*

The Alternative Conjunctions are:

*Principal—**or, nor***
*Associates—**else, otherwise***
*Correlatives—**either, neither, whether***

Either and *whether* are correlatives of *or*.

> Ex.—*I shall go either to-morrow or the day after.*
> *I do not know whether I shall go to-morrow or not.*

Neither is a correlative of *nor*.

> Ex.—*I shall go neither to-morrow nor the day after.*

Great care should be taken to avoid the use of *neither*, when *or* is the principal conjunction.

The member of the compound sentence introduced by an alternative conjunction is frequently elliptical.

> Ex.—*I shall go neither to-morrow nor (shall I go) the day after.*

Else is sometimes used alone, in the second member of a compound sentence, but *or* is always understood.

> Ex.—*Turn away from the path of the wicked; else it will lead you to destruction.*

When *whether* is used as a correlative of *or*, the negative following *or*, should be *not*. *No* is often incorrectly used in such sentences.

> Ex.—*Whether I shall go or not is uncertain.*

Otherwise is not often used in conversation, but it is found often in argumentative or didactic discourses.

> Ex.—*Your arguments must have the semblance of truth; otherwise they will not convince.*

MODEL.

Can Honor's voice provoke the silent dust,
Or Flattery soothe the dull, cold ear of death?

This is a *compound interrogative* sentence, consisting of two members.

Can Honor's voice provoke the silent dust, is the first member; *Or Flattery soothe the dull, cold ear of death?* is the second member.

Voice is the simple subject of the first member of the sentence; it is modified by *Honor's*, a simple adjective word element.

Can provoke	is the simple predicate; it is modified by *the silent dust*, a complex objective word element, modified by *silent*, a simple adjective word element; *silent dust* is modified by *the*, a simple adjective word element.
Flattery	is the subject of the second member; it is unmodified.
(Can) *Soothe*	is the simple predicate; it is modified by *the dull, cold ear of death*, a complex objective word element; *ear* is the basis, it is modified by *cold*, a simple adjective word element, and by *dull*, a simple adjective word element. Each of the elements, *dull* and *cold*, depends directly upon the word *ear*. *Ear* is modified, also, by *of death*, a simple adjective phrase element.
	Or is a coördinate alternative conjunction, used to join the two members of the compound sentence.

EXERCISES UPON COÖRDINATE ALTERNATIVE CLAUSES.

1. Canst thou bind the sweet influences of the Pleiades, or loose the bands of Orion?—BIBLE.

2. My lips shall not speak wickedness, nor my tongue utter deceit.

3. You must learn the value of time, or you will not succeed in any undertaking.

4. Obey your teacher, or suffer the consequences.

5. My tongue shall praise Thee continually, or be silent forevermore.

6. None of them can, by any means, redeem his brother, nor give to God a ransom for him.—BIBLE.

7. He is not a debtor to any man, nor does he intend to be.

8. Is it a foolish dream, an idle and vague superstition,
Or has an angel passed and revealed the truth to my spirit? —EVANGELINE.

CAUSAL COÖRDINATION.

The *second member* of a compound sentence sometimes expresses a *reason* for the statement made in the first member.

In such sentences, *for* is generally used as the connective.

Ex.—*Praise ye the Lord: for it is good to sing praises unto our God.*

For is frequently used at the *beginning* of a sentence; but it shows no grammatical relation to the preceding sentence; the relation is in thought only. Many such constructions are found in the Bible.

Ex.—*Enter not into the path of the wicked, and go not in the way of evil men.*
Avoid it; pass not by it, turn from it, and pass away.
For they sleep not, except they have done mischief.—BIBLE.

It will be seen, easily, that the sentence introduced by *For*, is related only in thought to what precedes.

When *for* is used to join two coördinate members of a sentence, they (the members) should be separated by a *semicolon*, if the coördination is close; but if the coördination is not very close, they should be separated by a colon.

MODEL.

Finish your work to-day; for I want you to go a fishing with me to-morrow.

This is a *compound* mixed sentence, consisting of two members.

The first member, *Finish your work to-day* is imperative.

The second member, *for I want you to go a fishing with me to-morrow*, is *declarative*, and it is, also, causal.

You (understood)	is the subject of the first member, it is unmodified.
Finish	is the simple predicate; it is modified by *your work*, a complex objective word element; *work* is the basis; it is modified by *your*, a simple adjective word element. *Finish* is modified, also, by *to-day* (on to-day) a simple adverbial phrase element of time.
I	is the subject of the second member, unmodified.
Want	is the simple predicate; it is modified by *you to go a fishing with me to-morrow*, a complex *double objective* element; *you* is the direct object, unmodified, *to go a*

fishing with me to-morrow, is the complex *attributive* object; *to go* is the basis, modified by *a fishing,* a simple adverbial phrase element denoting purpose (*a* is equivalent to *at*).

To go a fishing is modified by *with me,* a simple adverbial element of accompaniment; and, also, by *to-morrow,* a simple adverbial phrase element of time.

For is a coördinate *causal* conjunction, used to join the two members of the compound sentence.

EXERCISES UPON COÖRDINATE CAUSAL CLAUSES.

1. O give thanks to the Lord of lords; for his mercy endureth forever.

2. For a thousand years in thy sight are but as yesterday, when it is past, and as a watch in the night.

3. Nevertheless, the niece ate, the housekeeper drank, and Sancho Panza consoled himself; for legacies tend much to moderate the grief that nature claims for the deceased.

EMPHATIC COÖRDINATION AND MODELS FOR ANALYZING COMPOUND SENTENCES MADE EMPHATIC BY THE USE OF CORRELATIVES AND ASSOCIATE CONNECTIVES.

Copulative *coördination* is made emphatic by using with *and* the correlative *both,* and the following associates:

besides; likewise; moreover; therefore; then; further; furthermore; even; hence; wherefore also; so now.

And is often omitted, leaving the associate alone, as connective; and sometimes a sentence is introduced by an associate connective.

The use of the *associate* alone, is very common in the Bible, particularly at the beginning of a sentence.

    Ex.— *Wherefore*, also, we pray always for you, etc.
    Moreover, Job continued his parable, etc.
    Even to-day is my complaint better.
    Therefore they say unto God, Depart from us; for we desire not the knowledge of thy ways.

Adversative *coördination*, with *but* used to unite the members of a sentence, is not emphatic.

Adversative coördination is made emphatic by using the following associate connectives with *but:*

however, now, still, yet, notwithstanding, nevertheless, etc.

The associate of the adversative clause is frequently used alone, and sometimes introduces a sentence.

    Ex.—*Nevertheless my loving kindness will I not utterly take from him, nor suffer my faithfulness to fail.*

Alternative *coördination* with *or* is unemphatic; also, with *nor;* but with them are associated, for emphasis, *else* and *otherwise*. Emphasis is also given by using the correlative *either* and *whether* with *or*, and *neither*, with *nor*.

COMPOUND SENTENCES. 233

As in the case of copulative and of adversative coördination, the associate connective is often used alone; and sometimes it is used to introduce a sentence; the correlative is sometimes used alone also.

 Ex.—*I have none, else would I give it.*
 Dare to do right, otherwise your conduct will be cowardly.
 Neither is there any day's-man betwixt us that might lay his hand upon us both.—BIBLE.
 The topaz of Ethiopia shall not be equal to it, neither shall it be valued with pure gold.
           —BIBLE.

When coördinate conjunctions,—principal conjunctions, as: *and, but, or, nor*, or the associate connectives are used at the beginning of a sentence they indicate no grammatical union, but only coördination in thought.

Write sentences to illustrate emphatic coördinate constructions.

MODEL 1.

He both maintained the family by his labor, and besides he earned money enough to buy the neat little cottage where they live.

This is a *compound declarative* sentence, consisting of two members.

He both maintained the family by his labor is the first member of the sentence; *and besides he earned money enough to buy the neat little cottage where they live* is the second member.

 He   is the subject of the first member; it is unmodified.

10*

Maintained	is the simple predicate; it is modified by *the family*, a complex objective word element; *family* is the basis, modified by *the*, a simple adjective word element. *Maintained* is modified, also, by, *by his labor*, a complex adverbial phrase element, denoting manner; *by labor* is the basis; *labor* is modified by his, a simple adjective word element.
Both	is a conjunction; it is a correlative of *and;* it is used to make the coördination emphatic.
He	is the subject of the second member of the sentence; it is unmodified.
Earned	is the simple predicate; it is modified by *money enough to buy the neat little cottage where they live*, a complex objective word element; *money* is the basis; it is modified by *enough to buy the neat little cottage where they live*, a complex adjective word element; *enough* is the basis; it is modified by *to buy the neat little cottage where they live*, a complex adverbial phrase element of purpose; *to buy* is the basis; it is modified by *the neat little cottage where they live*, a complex objective word element; *cottage* is the basis; it is modified by *little*, a simple adjective word element; *little cottage* is modified by *neat*, a simple adjec-

tive word element; *neat little cottage* is modified by *the*, a simple adjective word element.

Cottage is modified, also, by *where they live*, a simple adjective clause element. *Where* is equivalent to *in which*.

They is the subject of the subordinate clause; it is unmodified.

Live is the simple predicate; it is modified by *where*, a simple adverbial element denoting place.

The members of the compound sentence are connected by *and*, a coördinate copulative conjunction, used to join parts of sentences that harmonize with each other; the coördination is strengthened by the associate connective *besides;* and by the correlative *both*, as seen above.

MODEL II.

In the days of his prosperity, he was a friend to the poor and the needy, and shall we not, therefore, aid him in the time of his adversity?

This is a *compound mixed* sentence.

The first member, *In the days of his prosperity, he was a friend to the poor and needy*, is declarative; the second member, *and shall we not, therefore, aid him in the time of his adversity?* is interrogative, a question of appeal.

He is the subject of the first member of the sentence ; it is unmodified.

Was friend is the predicate; *was* is the copula; *friend* is the substantive attribute, modified by *to the poor and the needy*, a compound adjective phrase element; *to poor* is the basis of the first member of the compound adjective element; *poor* is the basis, modified by *the*, a simple adjective word element.

(*To*) *needy* is the basis of the second member; *needy* is modified by *the*, a simple adjective word element.

And is a coördinate copulative conjunction, used to connect the members of the compound phrase element.

Was a friend to the poor and the needy, is modified by *in the days of his prosperity*, a complex adverbial phrase element denoting time; *in days* is the basis; *days* is modified by *the*, a simple adjective word element; and by *of his prosperity*, a a complex adjective phrase element; *of prosperity* is the basis; *prosperity* is modified by the adjective word element, *his*.

We is the subject of the second member of the sentence; it is unmodified.

Shall aid is the simple predicate; it is modified by *him,* a simple objective word element; and by *in the time of his adversity,* a complex adverbial phrase element; *in time* is the basis; *time* is modified by *the,* an adjective word element, and by *of adversity,* a simple adjective phrase element. The entire question is modified by *not* a model adverb.

And is a coördinate, copulative conjunction, used to connect the two members of the sentence.

Therefore is an associate connective, used with *and* to make the coördination emphatic; it is an illative conjunction, showing, or asking for, a consequence or conclusion to be drawn from the first member.

MODEL III.

E'en from the tomb the voice of nature cries,
E'en in our ashes live their wonted fires.

This is a *compound* sentence, consisting of two members, which are coördinate; and, as they harmonize, the construction is *copulative.* The conjunction is omitted.

E'en from the tombs the voice of nature cries, is the first member; *E'en in our ashes live their wonted fires,* is the second member.

Voice is the simple subject of the first member; it is modified by *the,* a simple adjective word element, and by *of nature,* a simple adjective phrase element.

Cries is the simple predicate. It is modified by *E'en from the tomb*, a complex adverbial phrase element of place; *from tomb*, is the basis; it is modified by *e'en* (even), a simple adverbial word element, used with *and* (understood) to make emphatic coördination with the preceding propositions. *From tomb* is the basis of the phrase element; *tomb* is modified by *the*, a simple adjective word element.

Fires is the simple subject of the second member of the compound sentence; it is modified by *wonted*, a simple adjective word element; *wonted fires* is modified by *their*, a simple adjective word element.

Live is the simple predicate; it is modified by *E'en in our ashes*, a complex adverbial element, denoting place; *in our ashes* is the basis, modified by *e'en* (even), an adverbial word element, used to give intensity to the meaning, and, also, with *and* understood, to make emphatic coördination. *In ashes* is the basis of the phrase, *ashes* is modified by *our*, a simple adjective word element.

MODEL IV.

Not only did I urge him to leave the country, but I also aided him, in every possible way, to do it.

This is a *compound declarative* sentence, consisting of two members.

Not only did I urge him to leave the country, is the first member; and *but I also aided him, in every way, to do it* is the second member.

I	is the subject of the first member; it is unmodified.
Did urge	is the simple predicate; it is modified by *him to leave the country*, a double objective element; *him* is the direct object; *to leave the country* is the attributive object; *to leave* is the basis, modified by *the country*, a complex objective word element; *country* is the basis, modified by *the*, a simple adjective word element.
I	is the subject of the second member; it is unmodified.
Aided	is the simple predicate; it is modified by *him*, a simple objective word element; and by *in every possible way*, a complex adverbial phrase element denoting manner; *in way* is the basis; *way* is modified by *possible*, a simple adjective word element; and *possible way* is modified by *every*, a simple adjective word element. *But* is here used as a coördinate copulative conjunction, uniting parts in harmony; *also* is an associate connective of *but*, used for the sake of emphasis, and *not only* is a correlative of *but*, used for the same purpose.

MODEL V.

½ of the more valuable ½ of his immense tract of land he has given you; but still you are not satisfied.

This is a *compound declarative* sentence, consisting of two members.

⅓ *of the more valuable* ½ *of his immense tract of land he has given you* is the first member; *but still you are not satisfied* is the second member.

He is the subject of the first member, unmodified.

Has given is the simple predicate, modified by ⅓ *of the more valuable* ½ *of his immense tract of land*, a complex direct objective word element; ⅓ is the basis; it is modified by *of the more valuable* ½ *of his immense tract of land*, a complex adjective phrase element; *of* ½ is the basis; it is modified by *more valuable*, a complex adjective word element; *valuable* is the basis, modified by the adverbial element *more*, used to denote the comparative degree; *more valuable* ½ is modified by *the*, a simple adjective word element; ½ is modified, also, by *of his immense tract of land*, a complex adjective phrase element; *of tract* is the basis; *tract* is modified by *immense*, a simple adjective word element; *immense tract* is modified by *his*, a simple adjective word element.

Tract is modified, also, by *of land*, a simple adjective phrase element.

You is the second member of the compound sentence, unmodified.

Are satisfied is the simple predicate; *are* is the copula and *satisfied* is the verbal attribute. The entire member of the sentence is modified by *not*, a modal negative adverb.

But is a coördinate adversative conjunction; *still* is used with *but* to give emphasis.

MODEL VI.

Neither did he see the messenger, nor did he receive the telegram.

This is a *compound declarative* sentence, consisting of two members.

Neither did he see the messenger, is the first member; *nor did he receive the telegram*, is the second member.

He is the subject of the first member; it is unmodified.

Did see is the simple predicate; it is modified by *the messenger*, a complex objective word element; *messenger* is the basis, modified by *the*, a simple adjective word element.

He is the subject of the second member; it is unmodified.

Did receive is the simple predicate; it is modified by *the telegram*, a complex objective word element; *telegram* is the basis, modified by *the*, a simple adjective word element. *Nor* is a coördinate alternative conjunction; *neither* is a correlative of *nor*, used for emphasis.

MODEL VII.

He either will leave to-morrow, or else he will remain a week longer.

This is a *compound declarative* sentence, consisting of two members.

He either will leave to-morrow, is the first member; *or else he will remain a week longer,* is the second member.

He — is the subject of the first member; unmodified.

Will leave — is the simple predicate; it is modified by (on) *to-morrow*, a simple adverbial phrase element.

He — is the subject of the second member, unmodified.

Will remain — is the simple predicate; it is modified by *a week longer*, a complex adverbial word element; *longer* is the basis; it is modified by (by) *a week*, a complex adverbial phrase element of duration of time; (by) *week* is the basis; *week* is modified by *a*, a simple adjective word element. The two members are connected by *or*, a coördinate alternative conjunction. The coördination is made emphatic by the associate conjunction *else*, and by the correlative *either*.

CONDENSED OR PARTIALLY COMPOUND SENTENCES.

RULE XIX.

When a sentence consists of a compound subject and a simple predicate, or a simple subject and a compound predicate, it should be called, in analysis, a partially compound sentence.

Language is often made more effective, and also more pleasing to the ear, by omitting parts which are common to the subject or to the predicate, or to any of the subordinate elements.

Repetitions should always be avoided, unless great emphasis is required.

Abbreviations are so numerous and so various, especially in conversation, that it would be difficult to give illustrations of all of them.

The student, however, will not find it difficult to supply omissions, if it be necessary to do so, in order to give a correct analysis of the sentence.

Ellipsis, or intentional omission, should be carefully distinguished from careless omission, and, also, from the abridgment of subordinate propositions.

Condensed sentences are sometimes called contracted compound sentences, sometimes abbreviated sentences, but the term commonly used is, *partially compound sentences.*

Those sentences only, whose subject, or predicate verb is compound, will be treated as *partially compound*.

Ex.—The moon and the stars shine by night.
The lark soars on high, and sings its morning song of praise.

MODEL I.

And further north, the priest stands at his door in the warm midnight, and lights his pipe with a common burning-glass.—LAND OF THE MIDNIGHT SUN.

This is a *contracted* (or partially compound) sentence, consisting of one subject and two predicates.

Priest   is the simple subject, modified by *the*, a simple adjective word element.

Stands and lights   is the compound predicate, without its modifiers. *Stands* is the first member of the compound predicate; it is modified by *at his door*, a complex adverbial phrase element of place; *at door* is the basis; *door* is modified by *his*, a simple adjective word element. *Stands* is modified also by *in the warm midnight*, a complex adverbial phrase element, denoting time; *in midnight* is the basis; *midnight* is modified by *warm*, a simple adjective word element; *warm midnight* is modified by *the*, a simple adjective word element.

Lights is the second member of the compound unmodified predicate; it is modified by *his pipe*, a complex objective word element (direct object); *pipe* is the basis, modified by *his*, a simple adjective word element.

Lights is modified also by *with a common burning-glass*, a complex adverbial phrase element of manner, denoting instrument; *with burning-glass* is the basis; *burning-glass* is modified by *common*, a simple adjective word element; *common burning-glass* is modified by *a*, a simple adjective word element.

MODEL II.

'Tis distance lends enchantment to the view,
And robes the mountain in its azure hue.—CAMPBELL.

This is a *complex declarative* sentence, consisting of one principal, and two subordinate propositions. *It is distance*, is the principal proposition; (*that*) *lends enchantment to the view, and* (*that*) *robes the mountain in its azure hue*, are the two subordinate propositions, which are coördinate with each other. In the analysis of this sentence it is necessary to supply ellipses, *it is*, for *'tis;* and *that*, as the subject of each subordinate proposition.

It   is the simple subject of the principal proposition; it is modified by (*that*) *lends enchantment to the view*, and (*that*) *robes the mountain in its azure hue*, a compound adjective clause element.

That   is the subject of the first subordinate clause; it is unmodified. (*That* is a relative pronoun, referring to *It* as antecedent; *It* represents the *thing*.

Lends   is the simple predicate; it is modified by *enchantment*, a simple objective word element, direct object; and by *to the view*, a complex objective phrase element, indirect object; *to view* is the basis; *view* is modified by *the*.

That   is the subject of the second subordinate clause, unmodified.

Robes   is the simple predicate; it is modified by *the mountain*, a complex objective word element; *mountain* is the basis; it is modified by *the*, a simple adjective word element. *Robes* is modified, also, by *in its azure hue*, a complex adverbial phrase element denoting manner; *in hue* is the basis; *hue* is modified by *azure*, a simple adjective word element; *azure hue* is modified by *its*, a simple adjective word element.

The two subordinate clauses are connected by *and*, a coördinate copulative conjunction.

EXERCISES UPON CONTRACTED COMPOUND SENTENCES.

1. Announced by all the trumpets of the sky,
Arrives the snow; and, driving o'er the fields,
Seems nowhere to alight. —EMERSON.

2. Of course, all good poetry descriptive of rural life is essentially pastoral, or has the effect of the pastoral, on the minds of men living in cities.—RUSKIN.

3. The prophet hears it, and leaves his cave.
—KRUMMACHER

4. The town of Pompeii was involved in the same dreadful catastrophe; but was not discovered till nearly forty years after the discovery of Herculaneum.
—KOTZEBUE.

5. She stopped where the cool spring bubbled up,
And filled for him her small tin cup.—WHITTIER.

6. And I'd feed the hungry, and clothe the poor.
—WHITTIER.

7. Long at the window he stood, and wistfully gazed at the landscape.—LONGFELLOW.

8. In the fisherman's cot, the wheel and the loom are still busy.—EVANGELINE.

9. Maidens still wear their Norman caps, and their kirtles of homespun,
And by the evening fire repeat Evangeline's story.
—EVANGELINE.

10. We forded a stream about four feet deep, and reached a sort of cave formed by boulders, where the Laplanders wanted to sleep.—LAND OF THE MIDNIGHT SUN.

11. The teachers and the pupils went, but did not remain very long.

12. They crossed the bridge, and turned up the stream, passing under an arch of stone, which serves as a gateway to this enchanted valley of Berkenau.—HYPERION.

13. Then shall He speak unto them in his wrath, and vex them in his sore displeasure.—BIBLE.

14. And all the rulers of the provinces, and the lieutenants, and the deputies and officers of the king, helped the Jews.—BIBLE.

15. My days are swifter than a weaver's shuttle, and are spent without hope.—JOB.

16. Governors and kings have little time to rest.

17. Sorrow and joy are impartial visitors.

18. She works and waits.

19. The sun and the moon give us light.

Let the pupil write original sentences predicating one thing of the following compound subjects.

> The sun, moon and stars;
> John and William;
> The boys and the girls;
> The preacher or the people;
> The air, the earth, and the water.

Write original sentences having simple subjects for the following compound predicates:

Writes and ciphers; plays and sings; studies and works; will be given and received; will be prolonged and blessed.

IDIOMATIC CONSTRUCTIONS.

Idiomatic expressions are *words*, *phrases* and *clauses* used out of their ordinary signification.

These *peculiar* constructions are abundant in the *English language*, to which many of them add *beauty* and *strength*, but, as they have entered into the language *regardless* of the *laws of syntax*, they will not yield to any method of analysis.

A few of these idiomatic constructions are given and the peculiarities pointed out.

1. I *had rather be* a dog and bay the moon than such a *Roman*.—SHAKESPEARE.

In this sentence, it is impossible *to show a relation* (of any kind) of *be* to *had*.

The origin of the expression is not known, but many consider it a corruption of *would;* and it would seem easy to change, by rapid utterance, *I would* to *I'd*, and that (*I'd*) to *I had*.

Rather is an adverb, used to denote preference.

The expressions *had rather*, *had better*, *had as well*, are used by the best writers and speakers.

2. *Woe worth* the day!—SCOTT.

This expression is only a *fragment* of a sentence; it cannot be analyzed.

Worth is from the *antiquated verb weorthan*, to become.

The expression means, *Let woe be to the day.*

3. I *was going to do it* when you came in.
4. I *went to move* the table and hurt my hand.

In the *first* of the foregoing sentences, *I was going to do it*, when used idiomatically, means, *I was just about to do it*, etc.

When the second sentence is used idiomatically it means, I *was attempting* to move the table, etc.

As it is *impossible* to show the relation of the infinitives in the sentences, to either *going* or to *went*, no satisfactory analysis is possible.

In the ordinary use of the words *going* and *went*, the infinitive denotes purpose.

I was going (*somewhere*) *for the purpose*, etc.
I went (*somewhere*) *for the purpose.*

5. ***How do you do*,** is another idiomatic expression, indispensable in our daily intercourse, but it cannot be satisfactorily analyzed. The word *do*, the last word in the expression, refers to the *state of health*, not to action.

As it has been said, the English language is *rich in idioms*, but they are too numerous to mention.

A language without idioms would be poor indeed.

Care should be taken to distinguish between an *idiomatic* expression and what is termed a *slang* expression.

Let the pupil find idiomatic expressions in the Reader, or in any other book.

MODELS OF ANALYSIS OF SENTENCES WITH PECULIAR CONSTRUCTION.

MODEL I.

*That you have wrong'd me, doth appear
In this :
You have condemned and noted Lucius Pella,
For taking bribes here of the Sardians;
Wherein my letters, praying on his side,
Because I knew the man, were slighted off.*
—SHAKESPEARE.

It is a *complex declarative* sentence, consisting of *four propositions:*

1. *That you have wrong'd me, doth appear in this.*

2. *You have condemned and noted Lucius Pella, For taking bribes here of the Sardians.*

3. *Wherein my letters, praying on his side, were slighted off.*

4. *Because I knew the man.*

That you have wronged me, doth appear in this, is the principal proposition.

That you have wrong'd me is a substantive clause, used as the subject of the principal proposition.

That is used simply to introduce the clause; it is not here a connective.

As subject, it should be disposed of as a noun, in the third person, singular number, neuter

You	gender, and in the nominative case, subject of *doth appear*. In analysis it may be resolved into its component parts. is the subject; it is unmodified.
Have wrong'd	is the simple predicate; it is modified by *me*, a simple objective word element (direct object).
Doth appear	is the simple predicate of the principal proposition; it is modified by *in this: You have condemned and noted Lucius Pella*, and all that follows, a complex adverbial phrase element; *in this* is the basis; *this* is modified by the four lines following,—a complex adjective clause element, by apposition.
You	is the subject of the first subordinate proposition; it is not modified.
Have condemned and noted	is the compound predicate; it is modified by *Lucius Pella*, a simple objective word element. *Have condemned and noted Lucius Pella*, is modified by *For taking bribes here of the Sardians*, a complex adverbial phrase element, denoting a

cause or reason; *For taking* is the basis (*taking* is a present active participle, used as a noun in the objective after *For*, but modified as a verb); *taking* is modified by *bribes*, a simple objective word element (direct object), and by *of the Sardians*, a complex objective phrase element (indirect object); *taking* is modified also by *here*, a simple adverbial element of place. The entire expression, *You have condemned and noted Lucius Pella, For taking bribes here of the Sardians*, is modified by *Wherein my letters, praying on his side, Because I knew the man, were slighted off*, a complex adjective clause element. *Wherein* is a relative adverb, equivalent to *concerning which*, and relates to what is in the two lines preceding.

Letters is the simple subject; it is modified by *my*, a simple adjective word element; and by *praying on his side, Because I knew the man*, a complex adjective word element, participial construction; *praying* is the basis; it is modified by *on his side*, a complex adverbial phrase element place; *on side* is the basis; *side* is modified by *his*, a simple adjective word element.

Praying on his side is modified by *Because I knew the man*, an adverbial clause element, denoting a cause or a reason.

I is the subject, unmodified.

Knew is the simple predicate; it is modified by *the man*, a complex objective word element (direct object); *man* is the basis; it is modified by *the*, a simple adjective word element.

Were slighted off is the predicate; it is that which is affirmed of *letters;* it is unmodified.

The predicate consists of the copula *were*, and the verbal attribute, *slighted off*. *Were slighted off* is a compound verb. *Off* should not be separated from the verb, in analysis or in parsing.

Because is a causal conjunction, used as a connective, to join the subordinate clause to the element which it modifies.

MODEL II.

The performance was not worth seeing.

This is a *simple declarative sentence.*

Performance is the simple subject; it is modified by *the*, a simple adjective word element.

Was worth is the simple predicate; *was* is the copula, and *worth* is the adjective attribute. *Worth* is modified by *seeing* (a participial noun) an indirect objective element.

NOTE.— *Worth* is followed by an indirect object, with no preposition expressed when it (*worth*) is used as an adjective.

MODEL III.

On my honor, I have told you all.

This is a *simple declarative* sentence.

I is the subject, unmodified.

Have told is the simple predicate; it is modified by *all*, a simple direct objective word element; and by *you*, a simple objective phrase element, indirect object.

On my honor is used by way of asseveration, to give emphasis to the expression.

MODEL IV.

For he saith to the snow, Be thou on the earth; likewise to the small rain, and to the great rain of his strength.—BIBLE.

This is a *complex mixed* sentence; the *principal proposition* is *declarative;* the *subordinate proposition* is *imperative.*

He saith to the snow, likewise to the small rain, and to the great rain of his strength is the principal proposition.

Be thou on the earth is the subordinate proposition, though it is really the leading thought; it is subordinate, only because it is a direct quotation.

He   is the subject of the principal proposition, unmodified.

Saith   is the simple predicate; it is modified by *Be thou on the earth*, a simple direct objective clause element.

Thou   is the subject, unmodified.

Be   is the simple predicate; it is used to denote existence; it is modified by *on the earth*, a complex adverbial phrase element denoting place; *on earth* is the basis; *earth* is modified by *the*, a simple adjective word element. *Saith* is modified also by *to the snow, likewise to the small rain, and to the great rain of his strength*, a compound objective phrase element; *to the snow* is the first member; *to snow* is the basis; *snow* is modified by *the*. *Likewise to the small rain* is the second member; *to rain* is the basis; *rain* is modified by *small*, a simple adjective word element. *Small rain* is modified by *the*, a simple adjective word element. The second member of the phrase element is connected to the first by *likewise*, generally used as an associate of *and*, but here it may be regarded as a real connective (coördinate copulative conjunction), though *and* may be supplied.

And to the great rain of his strength is the third member of the objective phrase element, joined to the second by the coördinate copulative conjunction *and; to rain* is the basis; *rain* is modified by *great*, a simple adjective word element; *great rain* is modified by *the*, a simple adjective word element; *rain* is modified also by *of his strength*, a complex adjective phrase element.

Be thou on the earth is the prominent thought in the sentence, and is subordinate in construction, only because it is direct quotation, a part of what was said.

MODEL V.

Long Indian canes, with iron tipped they bear,
And upon steeds so nimbly sweep along,
You'd say a whirlwind blew them past. —Tasso.

This is a *complex* sentence; the principal proposition is partially compound, containing one subject and two predicate verbs.

Long Indian canes, with iron tipped they bear, And upon steeds so nimbly sweep along, is the principal proposition.

You'd say a whirlwind blew them past, is the subordinate complex proposition.

They is the subject of the principal proposition, unmodified.

Bear is the first member of the compound predicate; it is modified by *Long Indian canes, with iron tipped*, a complex objective word element. *Canes* is the basis, modified by *Indian*, a simple adjective word element; *Indian canes* is modified by *Long*, a simple adjective element. *Canes* is modified, also, by *with iron tipped*, a complex adjective word element, participial construction; *tipped* is the basis, modified by *with iron*, a simple adverbial phrase element of manner.

Sweep along is the second member of the compound predicate. (*Along* is a preposition usually, but it enters into and changes the meaning of the verb *sweep* so materially that with it (*sweep*), it forms a compound verb.

Sweep along is modified by *upon steeds*, a simple adverbial phrase element of manner, and by *so nimbly*, a complex adverbial word element denoting manner; *nimbly* is the basis, modified by *so*, a simple adverbial word element of degree.

Nimbly is modified, also, by *You'd say a whirlwind blew them past*, a complex adverbial clause element denoting consequence.

That should be supplied before *you*, and before *a whirlwind*,—*That you would say that a whirlwind blew them past*

You is the subject of the first subordinate proposition, unmodified.

Would say is the simple predicate; it is modified by *that a whirlwind blew them past*, a simple objective clause element.

Whirlwind is the simple subject of the objective clause, modified by *a*, a simple adjective word element.

Blew is the simple predicate; it is modified by *them*, a simple objective word element; and by *past*, a simple adverbial word element.

So is not only an adverb of degree, but is also a correlative of *that*, the subordinate conjunction (understood) connecting the clause element to the adverb *nimbly*.

That is understood also, before the last clause.

MODEL VI.

*Then methought the air grew denser, perfumed from an
unseen censer,
Swung by angels, whose faint footfalls tinkled on the tufted
floor.* —POE.

This is a *complex declarative* sentence. The subject is a clause, which contains another clause used as a modifier.

Then methought (*that* understood) *the air grew denser, perfumed from an unseen censer, swung by angels,* is the principal proposition; *whose faint footfalls tinkled on the tufted floor,* is the subordinate proposition.

That the air grew denser, perfumed from an unseen censer,
Swung by angels, is the simple subject.

Thought is the simple predicate; it is modified by *to me,* an indirect objective phrase element.

Thought, in *methought*, is derived from *thincan, to seem, to appear,* and not from *thencan, to think*.

Air is the simple subject of the substantive *clause subject;* it is modified by *the,* a simple adjective word element, and by *perfumed from an unseen censer, swung by angels, whose faint footfalls tinkled on the tufted floor*, a complex adjective word element, participial construction.

Perfumed is the basis; it is modified by *from an unseen censer, swung by angels, whose faint footfalls tinkled on the tufted floor*, a complex adverbial phrase element denoting place; *from censer* is the basis; *censer* is modified by *unseen*, a simple adjective word element; *unseen censer* is modified by *an*, a simple adjective word element. *Censer* is modified, also, by *swung by angels, whose faint footfalls tinkled on the tufted floor*, a complex adjective word element, participial construction. *Swung* is the basis; it is modified by, *by angels whose faint footfalls tinkled on the tufted floor*, a complex adverbial phrase element denoting agency; *by angels* is the basis; *angels* is modified by *whose faint footfalls tinkled on the tufted floor*, a simple adjective clause element

Footfalls	is the simple subject of the subordinate clause; it is modified by *faint*, a simple adjective word element; *faint footfalls* is modified by *whose*, a simple adjective word element.
Tinkled	is the simple predicate; it is modified by *on the tufted floor*, a complex adverbial phrase element, of place; *on floor* is the basis; *floor* is modified by *tufted*, a simple adjective word element.
Grew denser	is the predicate of the clause used as subject (it is predicated of air). *Grew* is a copulative verb, used to connect the adjective attribute *denser* to the subject *air*.

EXERCISES ON SENTENCES CONTAINING METHINKS.

1. Methinks that the stars look down pityingly upon this scene of sorrow.

2. Methought there was a proclamation made by Jupiter, that every mortal should bring in his griefs and calamities, and throw them together in a heap.—ADDISON.

3. And methought that the light-house looked lovely as as Hope,
   That Star on life's tremulous ocean.
—MOORE.

MODEL VII.

From peak to peak, the rattling crags among,
Leaps the live thunder.   —BYRON.

This sentence is transposed, for rhetorical effect; the elements are inverted or placed out of their natural order. It is a *simple declarative* sentence.

The live thunder leaps among the crags, from peak to peak, is the natural order of arrangement.

Thunder   is the simple subject; it is limited by *live*, a simple adjective word element; *live thunder* is limited by *the*, a simple adjective word element.

Leaps   is the simple predicate; it is modified by *among the crags*, a complex adverbial phrase element, denoting place; *among crags* is the basis; *crags* is modified by *the*, an adjective word element. *Leaps* is modified also by *from peak to peak*, a complex adverbial phrase element, of manner, showing how the thunder leaps among the crags; and it also refers to place. *From peak* is the basis; it is modified by *to peak*, a simple adverbial phrase element.

MODEL FOR ANALYZING A COMPLEX INTERROGATIVE SENTENCE.

Who laid the corner-stone thereof;
When the morning-stars sang together,
and all the sons of God shouted for joy?

This is a *complex interrogative* sentence, consisting of three propositions, one principal and two subordinate propositions.

Who laid the corner-stone thereof, is the principal proposition; *When the morning-stars sang together* is the first subordinate proposition; (when) *all the sons of God shouted for joy* is the second.

The two subordinate propositions are coördinate with each other.

Who is the subject of the principal proposition; it is also an interrogative pronoun, used to inquire for an antecedent, which is found in the answer; it is unmodified.

Laid is the simple predicate; it is modified by *the corner-stone thereof*, a complex objective word element; *corner-stone* is the basis; it is modified by *thereof*, a simple adjective word element, equivalent to *of it*. *Laid the corner-stone thereof* is modified by *When the morning-stars sang together, and (when) all the sons of God shouted for joy*, a compound adverbial clause element denoting time simultaneous. The two clauses are connected by the coördinate copulative conjunction *and*.

Morning-stars is the simple subject (it is a compound word); it is modified by *the*, a simple adjective word element.

Sang is the simple predicate; it is modified by *together*, a simple adjective

Sons is the simple subject of the second member of the compound subordinate clause element; it is modified by *the*, a simple adjective word element; *the sons* is modified by *all*, a simple adjective word element; *sons* is modified, also, by *of God*, a simple adjective phrase element.

word element, denoting accompaniment; and by *when*, an adverbial word element, denoting time.

Shouted is the simple predicate; it is modified by *for joy*, a simple adverbial phrase element denoting the cause or reason.

MODEL FOR OUTLINE ANALYSIS.

I.

Of Man's first disobedience, and the fruit
Of that forbidden tree, whose mortal taste
Brought death into the world, and all our woe,
With loss of Eden, till one greater Man
Restore us, and regain the blissful seat,
Sing, heavenly Muse, that on the secret top
Of Oreb, or of Sinai, didst inspire
That shepherd, who first taught the heavenly seed,
In the beginning how the heavens and earth
Rose out of chaos:

This is the *first member* of the compound sentence which is the opening sentence of Paradise Lost; but it will be disposed of as one entire sentence.

It is a *complex imperative* sentence; the following is the natural order of arrangement:

1. ***Heavenly Muse,***	Independent by address.
2. ***That on the secret top of Oreb or of Sinai didst inspire that shepherd,***	Basis of the complex adjective clause element which modifies *Muse;* this element contains three clauses.
3. ***Who first taught the heavenly seed, In the beginning***	is the subordinate adjective clause, used to limit *shepherd;* it is a complex adjective clause; *taught* is modified by *How the heavens and earth Rose out of chaos,* an objective clause element.

All given above is independent by direct address. It has no grammatical relation, whatever, to the sentence, though closely connected in thought.

4. ***Thou*** (understood)	Subject.
5. ***Sing***	Predicate Verb

6. *Of Man's first disobedience and the fruit of the forbidden tree,*   Basis of the complex objective phrase element.

7. *Whose mortal taste brought death into the world, with loss of Eden,*   Adjective clause element, used to modify *fruit.*
   With loss of Eden, an adverbial element of accompaniment.

8. *Till one greater man restore us and regain the blissful seat.*   Compound adverbial element of time.

MODEL II.

At summer eve, when Heaven's ethereal bow
Spans with bright arch the glittering hills below,
Why to yon mountain turns the musing eye,
Whose sunbright summit mingles with the sky?

It is a *complex interrogative* sentence. It is an *inverted* sentence. The following is the natural order of arrangement.

Why   Interrogative adverb, used to ask for a cause or reason.

The musing eye   Subject with modifiers.

Turns   Simple predicate.

To yon mountain whose sunbright summit mingles with the sky,	Adverbial phrase element denoting direction, complex; modifying *turns*.
Whose sunbright summit mingles with the sky,	Subordinate adjective clause element, modifying mountain and forming a part of the complex adverbial phrase element of direction.
At summer eve	Adverbial phrase element of time, modifying *turns*.
When Heaven's ethereal bow spans with bright arch the glittering hills below	A complex adjective clause element (*when* is equivalent to *at which time*), used to modify *eve*.
Below	is an adjective element, belonging to *hills*, equivalent to *which are below it*.

EXERCISES FOR PUPILS.

Construct five sentences, arrange the words in natural order, then change to the inverted order.

Find inverted sentences in a Reader, and arrange the words in natural order.

Let the pupils arrange the words in the following sentences, in their natural order, and then analyze the sentences:

EXERCISES.

1. Far down the Beautiful River,
    Past the Ohio shore, and past the mouth of the Wabash,
    Into the golden stream, of the broad, and swift Mississippi,
    Floated a cumbrous boat, that was rowed by Acadian boatmen. —LONGFELLOW.

2. As boys on ivied towers and haunted rooms
    At fall of twilight dare not cast an eye,
    Fancy a ghost in everything that glooms,
    And, hair on end, from the grim fancy fly;
    So when beyond the hills these men descry
    The hoar wood nodding to the winds light wings,
    Alarmed, they turn and flee. —TASSO.

3. Once upon a midnight dreary, while I pondered weak and weary,
    Over many a quaint and curious volume of forgotten love,
    While I nodded, nearly napping, suddenly there came a tapping. —POE.

4.   When thoughts
Of the last bitter hour come like a blight,
Over thy spirit, and sad images
Of the stern agony, and shroud, and pall,
And breathless darkness, and the narrow house,
Make thee to shudder, and grow sick at heart,
Go forth, under the open sky, and list
To Nature's teaching. —BRYANT.

MODEL FOR ANALYZING EXCLAMATORY SENTENCES.

How beautiful was the hour of midnight!
  —LAND OF THE MIDNIGHT SUN.

This is a *simple exclamatory* sentence; it is expressive of strong admiration.

Hour is the simple subject, modified by *the*, a simple adjective word element, and by *of midnight*, a simple adjective phrase element.

Was beautiful is the simple predicate; *was* is the copula; and *beautiful* is the adjective attribute. The attribute, *beautiful*, is modified by *how*, a simple adverbial word element of degree, used also to indicate emotion.

EXERCISES UPON EXCLAMATORY SENTENCES.

1. O solitude! where are the charms that sages have seen in thy face!
2. What a delightful day!
3. Oh had I known it sooner!

EXERCISES.

4. Oh for a lodge in some vast wilderness!

5. Alas, what have I done!

6. How drowsy was the landscape!

7. Alas for him who never sees
The stars shine through his cypress trees!
—WHITTIER.

8. Boys, a path!—WHITTIER.

9. Therefore accomplish thy labor of love till the heart is made Godlike,
Purified, strengthened, perfected, and rendered more worthy of Heaven! —LONGFELLOW.

10. Ah well! for us all some sweet hope lies
Deeply buried from human eyes.

11. And, in the hereafter, angels may
Roll the stone from its grave away!
—WHITTIER.

12. How beautiful upon the mountains are the feet of him that bringeth good tidings, that publisheth peace!
—BIBLE.

FINIS.

INDEX.

	PAGE		PAGE
A or an	86	Expletive	78, 79
A fishing	230	False Syntax	9
Abridged propositions	191	For, preposition	62, 83
participial constructions	192-203	subordinate conjunction	159
infinitive constructions	204	co-ordinate conjunction	209, 211, 229
Adjective	38	Had rather	249
pronominal	38, 39	Harmony	209, 210
numeral	39, 41	Idiomatic constructions	249, 250
qualifying	41, 43	Ill	74
Adjective element	34	Illative clause	235, 237
word	34-54	Imperative sentence	16
phrase	56	In, into	85
clause	116-123	Indefinite article	86
Adverbs	71	Infinitives	29, 56, 86-90
time	72	present and perfect, when to be used	205
place	72	special uses	204
cause	73	Interrogative sentences	16, 205
manner	73	Intransitive verbs	59
Adverbial element	71	It, expletive	99
word	71-80	Like	78, 79
phrase	81, 90	Many a	87
clause	136-191	Methought	250
Adversative conjunctions	221	Modal adverbs	75, 76, 77
Ago	78	Mixed sentence	17
Alternative conjunctions	226	Neither	39, 226
Along	85	Nor	226, 249
Analysis	19	Not	77, 185
And	209	Not only	210, 236
Apposition	48, 49, 123	Numerals	39
Appeal	90	Oath	90
As, adverb of degree	163	Objective element	56
conjunction	136, 156	direct object	57
relative pronoun	108	indirect object	60-63
Asseveration	90, 255	double object	64-67
At	85	objective clause	127
Attribute, word	21-25	or, otherwise	226, 227
phrase	27-30	Ought	47
clause	101	Participles	43, 47
Bad, badly	33	Phrase	27, 55
Be, uses of the verb	19	Possessives	50-53
to denote existence	20-21	Predicate	10-11
as copula	21-25	Proposition	9
Both, conjunction	233	Quotations	129
But, conjunction	209	Relative Adverbs	118-123
preposition	128, 147	Relative pronouns	106-118
relative pronoun	108, 109	Rules of Analysis	94, 96
Causal clause and causal coordination	150, 229	Rules of Syntax	92-94
Clause element	97	Sentence, defined	
Complex sentences	105	simple	17
Compound sentences	209-242	complex	105
Condensed sentences	243-248	compound	209
Conjunctions, co-ordinate	209, 231, 232	Subject	10-11, 96, 104
Copula	21-25	Syntax	9
Copulative verbs	30, 34, 64	Than	163
Copulative conjunctions	209	That, conjunction	129, 130
Correlatives	110	pronominal adjective	38
Comparison of equality	152	relative pronoun	107
negative equality	152	The, definite article	87
inequality	155	The—the	176
Declarative sentence	15	There	78, 113
Definite article	86	Thought, a	9
Discourse	129	To, toward, towards	87
direct	129	Transitive verb	57, 58
indirect	129	Voice	58
During	82	Well	74
Either	39, 226	What	108
Elements	12, 14	Whence	152
Else	227, 237	Whether	227
Even	237	Whither	152
Exclamatory sentence	16-17	Worth	249, 255

www.ingramcontent.com/pod-product-compliance
Lightning Source LLC
Chambersburg PA
CBHW031952230426
43672CB00010B/2137